D1226364

The Titanic Story

by Tristan Poehlmann

Content Consultant

Sheryl Rinkol

Titanic Teacher and Presenter

Famous *Ships*

Essential Library

An Imprint of Abdo Publishing | abdopublishing.com

abdopublishing.com

Published by Abdo Publishing, a division of ABDO, PO Box 398166, Minneapolis, Minnesota 55439. Copyright © 2018 by Abdo Consulting Group, Inc. International copyrights reserved in all countries. No part of this book may be reproduced in any form without written permission from the publisher. Essential Library™ is a trademark and logo of Abdo Publishing.

Printed in the United States of America, North Mankato, Minnesota
102017
012018

THIS BOOK CONTAINS RECYCLED MATERIALS

Cover Photo: PA Wire URN:5716301/Press Association/AP Images
Interior Photos: Everett Historical/Shutterstock Images, 4–5, 18–19, 25, 70–71, 79, 80–81; Bain News Service/George Grantham Bain Collection/Library of Congress, 8, 22–23, 88–89; iStockphoto, 11; John S. Johnston/Detroit Publishing Company/Library of Congress, 12–13; Pach Bros./Library of Congress, 20; George Grantham Bain Collection/Library of Congress, 29, 56; World History Archive/Alamy, 32–33, 47; IanDagnall Computing/Alamy, 36; Science Source, 38; Engineering journal: 'The White Star liner *Titanic*', vol.91., 40–41; Anton Ivanov/Shutterstock Images, 42–43; Carl Simon/United Archives GmbH/Alamy, 48–49; Red Line Editorial, 50, 73, 85, 97; Frilet Patrick/hemis.fr/Hemis/Alamy, 52–53; Stephen Barnes/Alamy, 59; Shutterstock Images, 61; Roger Viollet/Getty Images, 62–63; Adrio Communications Ltd/Shutterstock Images, 65; Universal Images Group/Getty Images, 67; Chronicle/Alamy, 75; Interfoto/History/Alamy, 86; movies/Alamy, 91; Library of Congress, 94

Editor: Heather C. Hudak
Series Designer: Craig Hinton

Publisher's Cataloging-in-Publication Data

Names: Poehlmann, Tristan, author.
Title: The Titanic story / by Tristan Poehlmann.
Description: Minneapolis, Minnesota : Abdo Publishing, 2018. | Series: Famous ships | Includes online resources and index.
Identifiers: LCCN 2017946750 | ISBN 9781532113215 (lib.bdg.) | ISBN 9781532152092 (ebook)
Subjects: LCSH: Titanic (Steamship)--History--Juvenile literature. | Shipwrecks--Juvenile literature. | North Atlantic Ocean--Juvenile literature.
Classification: DDC 910.9163--dc23
LC record available at https://lccn.loc.gov/2017946750

Contents

⚓ *In 1912, the* Titanic *struck an iceberg and sank on its maiden voyage.*

Chapter 1

ABANDON SHIP!

The pitch-black night of the northern Atlantic Ocean was lit by a starry sky, and the massive deck of the RMS *Titanic* swarmed with confused passengers and crew members. Electric lamps shone out from row upon row of portholes that should have been dark. It was nearly one o'clock in the morning, and the ship's passengers should have been in bed.

Charlotte Collyer stood at the ship's railing, shivering as her gaze moved between the dark sea below and the milling crowd. The sea was calm and still, and the cold air was sharp. Surely nothing serious could have gone wrong with the ship, she thought. It was so large,

How Did an Iceberg Sink the Titanic?

Only a fraction of an iceberg is visible above the waterline; approximately 90 percent is underwater.[1] This hidden portion of the iceberg is what damaged the *Titanic*—but not necessarily by ripping a hole in it, as many people assume. Instead, one theory suggests it was pressure that caused the hull to break. As the ship turned to avoid a head-on collision with the iceberg, its side was pushed so hard against the iceberg that a section of its hull crumpled, causing the rivets that bound the hull together to pop off. Without rivets, the steel panels that made up the hull began to split apart. Ocean water rushed into the ship through these gaps, eventually sinking it.

she felt just as safe as if she were standing on land. So why were the officers calling women and children to the lifeboats?

On the Open Ocean

The voyage from Southampton in England had been uneventful for Collyer and her husband, Harvey. Their young daughter, Marjorie, was seasick during the first three days on the ocean. They kept to their cabin rather than exploring the palatial ship. But this morning Marjorie had felt somewhat better, able to eat the fancy Sunday dinner served in the second-class dining room and listen to the musicians play after dinner.

Inside their cozy cabin that evening, Collyer and her husband rested as the *Titanic* sped across the cold ocean. Sometime just before midnight, they felt the ship make a sudden jerk. Collyer sat up in bed. Her husband stumbled where he stood. They both listened closely.

The engines seemed to have stopped, and the silence sounded strange. After a moment, the engines rumbled as if starting up again but then died back. The massive ship lay still.

Out on the deck at around 12:45 a.m., Collyer and her husband were still unsure what had occurred. No one they talked to appeared seriously worried, not even the officers calling for the lifeboats to be loaded. "There's no danger," they reassured the women passengers, trying to coax them into the boats.[2]

Collyer held onto Marjorie's hand and stayed close to her husband. She didn't want to be separated from him and lowered down into the black ocean in a small boat. She felt much safer on the deck. As they watched, distress flares shot up from the ship and burst in the sky like firecrackers. Clearly, there was some problem, Collyer argued with herself, but it couldn't be urgent. No one seemed able to explain why the ship was signaling for help.

Suddenly, a man covered in coal dust lurched out of a nearby passageway. He was a stoker, Collyer realized, one of the workers from the boiler rooms at the very bottom of the ship who shoveled coal for the engines. Something must have happened down there, she thought—an accident. He stumbled to a stop as Collyer called, "Is there any danger?"

"Danger!" he cried. "It's hell down below. This boat will sink like a stone in ten minutes!"[3]

Collyer grasped her husband's arm tightly in shock. A sickening fear rose in her throat.

⚓ *Charlotte Collyer and her daughter, Marjorie, survived the sinking of the* Titanic.

Disaster

As the minutes ticked by, the ship began to tilt. Through the passageways, third-class passengers finally found the way up from their cabins in steerage. They began to pour out onto the deck, clutching their possessions. Their faces were grim and frightened.

"Lower the boats!"[4] The officer's cry pricked goosebumps on Collyer's skin, but she held onto her husband's arm, unwilling to leave him.

A sailor grabbed Marjorie away from Collyer, tossing the child into the nearest lifeboat. "You're a woman," he yelled at Collyer. "Take a seat in that boat or it will be too late!"[5]

The solid deck seemed to be slipping away under Collyer's feet. "Go, Lottie, for God's sake, be brave and go!" her husband urged. "I'll get a seat in another boat."[6]

Before she could answer, the sailor yanked her toward the lifeboat and pushed her in, and the rushing crowd closed in behind her. Collyer got to her feet and glimpsed her husband's back as he turned and strode away down the deck.

Why Weren't There Enough Lifeboats?

The *Titanic* carried only enough lifeboats to evacuate one-half of its passengers. At the time, this was not uncommon for an ocean liner. In fact, the *Titanic* carried more lifesaving equipment than regulations required. The regulations governing lifeboats were based on gross registered tonnage of the vessel. Ships built using newer technology were often much larger. The lifeboat laws were outdated as a result. Also, many people believed the larger ships were safer. However, this was not necessarily true. Additionally, most of the lifeboats were launched before they reached full capacity. This is why, although half of the *Titanic*'s passengers could have been rescued, only one-third of them survived.

He will find another boat, she comforted herself as the lifeboat lowered. She shuddered and wrapped an arm around her daughter as the small boat smacked down into the sea.

What Happened?

In the early hours of April 15, 1912, the *Titanic* broke in half and then plunged to the bottom of the Atlantic Ocean. Approximately 2,200 people were on board the ship. Only 700 people survived.[7]

More than 100 years later, the *Titanic* disaster remains perhaps the most famous shipwreck of all time. Because nobody seemed to believe the ship would sink, it is often remembered as a lesson in hubris—the arrogance of humanity in thinking itself invincible, which leads to its doom. But were the people on board the *Titanic* arrogant? Were the captain and crew? Were the people who built, designed, or financed the ship? Was the *Titanic* doomed to fail?

Rediscovering the Titanic

For more than 70 years, no one knew precisely where the *Titanic* landed on the ocean floor. Its final resting place, as well as its condition, was a mystery. Then, in 1985, explorer Dr. Robert Ballard located the shipwreck using submersible robots he developed for deep-sea research. It was a stunning discovery that led to a resurgence of interest in the story of the *Titanic*, and Dr. Ballard's work was featured on the cover of *Time* magazine.

⚓ *RMS* Teutonic *was in service from 1889 to 1920.*

Chapter 2

THE GROWTH OF THE OCEAN LINER

*I*n 1889, 20 years before building the *Titanic*, the British shipping company White Star Line launched the world's first modern ocean liners. The *Teutonic* and the *Majestic* were a new kind of ship for a new kind of market. Run entirely on steam power, the ocean liners looked very different from previous models—they were huge ships without sails.

Transatlantic Trade

Although steam engines had powered Britain's industry for decades, the development of steamships able to cross the Atlantic Ocean took some time. It was, however, a key investment for shipping companies. Since the 1860s, the British shipping market had grown significantly, due in large part to the United States. In the last half of the 1800s, trade between Britain and the United States increased 700 percent as the population of the United States grew 400 percent.[1]

The cargo carried across the ocean was dominated by cotton, tobacco, and wheat. These products were part of a growing, complex international industrialized economy. For example, cotton grown in the United States by sharecroppers, often formerly enslaved people, was then shipped to Britain for processing in a cotton mill, where women and children typically worked the machinery. This kind of international economy made shipping a very profitable business.

This boom in transatlantic trade was one major factor in the development of ocean liners, but another was the increase in European emigration. The growth of the US population was driven by immigrants arriving from all over Europe, most of them traveling on third-class tickets. Steerage, as it was known, was the cheapest ticket to the United States, and as demand grew, shipping companies looked for ways to capitalize on it. More space for passengers was necessary in order to earn the maximum profit per passage. Larger, faster ocean liners seemed to be the wave of the future. "Steamships of the monster type," as the chairman of the White Star Line once wrote, were the inevitable result.[2]

Developing the Technology

The Industrial Revolution literally changed the landscape of Britain during the 1800s, spreading economic change outward from major cities, such as London and Liverpool, into the countryside. Railroads were perhaps the most visible aspect of this change, their tracks extending from town to town, transporting people and manufactured products. But along with the growth of the railroads came the evolution of other steam-driven transportation.

The coal-powered steam engine, the backbone of the Industrial Revolution, had been constantly

Steam Turbines Powered Ocean Liners

Invented by Charles Parsons in 1884, the steam turbine was a type of steam engine that could operate at much higher speeds than a typical steam engine. A typical steam engine used the pressure of hot steam to push a piston, which, in turn, drove a wheel connected to a machine that performed work. The new design of the steam turbine used rotating blades similar to windmills rather than the up-and-down piston motion of the steam engine. Pushing steam through a series of rotating blades took up less space, moved faster, and created more pressure, allowing for smaller engines as well as greater production of power. Giant steam turbines, such as those on ocean liners, could produce enough power for ships to travel at speeds previously unimaginable.

evolving since the late 1700s. River-going steamboats were increasingly common through the early 1800s, but it wasn't until the 1830s that steamships for the open ocean were considered technologically feasible. The SS *Great Western*, launched in 1837, was the first steamship built for service on the North Atlantic Ocean, and its design proved that large ocean liners were an economic possibility.

New work in mechanical engineering showed that as the size of a ship increased, the percentage of the ship needed for fuel storage decreased, creating more room for cargo and passengers. This realization led many shipping companies to invest in the development of steamship technology and engineering. By the early 1900s, when powerful steam turbines revolutionized ship design, the intense competition reached new heights.

Bigger, Better, Faster

The transatlantic shipping industry was dominated by a handful of companies, and in Britain, the most successful were the White Star Line and the Cunard Line. Throughout the late 1800s and into the early 1900s, these two companies engaged in fierce competition. Vying to engineer bigger and faster ships to maximize profits, the companies traded the lead in cutting-edge technology for decades.

When the United States entered the competition, the stakes were raised even higher. After the end of the American Civil War (1861–1865), shipping boomed and J. P. Morgan, an American financier, made it his goal to build a transatlantic shipping monopoly. Buying up British and German shipping companies, he was able to reduce competition, lowering the price of steerage tickets until other companies had to engage in a price war to attract passengers. Morgan's main goal was to force the Cunard Line to accept his buyout offer, but this ultimately failed. However, in 1902 he succeeded in gaining control of the White Star Line and making it part of his International Mercantile Marine Company, a group of shipping companies he controlled.

In 1907, the Cunard Line launched two new ships, the *Lusitania* and the *Mauretania*. They were larger and faster than any other ships running and quickly became famous and beloved symbols of technological progress.

White Star Line

Thomas Ismay took ownership of the White Star Line in 1868, growing it from bankruptcy to one of the most successful shipping companies of its time. Aware of the growing market of transatlantic emigrants, the White Star Line was one of the first companies to offer third-class, or steerage, accommodations, along with first- and second-class accommodations. When Thomas Ismay died in 1899, his son, Bruce, took over the business. But in 1902, Bruce lost his sole control of it when J. P. Morgan, an American financier, invested in the company and made it part of the International Mercantile Marine Company (IMMC). The White Star Line remained under Ismay's chairmanship due to growing tensions between the United States and Britain over economic dominance on the world stage. The year after the *Titanic* disaster, the White Star Line posted record profits, and the company continued to do well financially for many years.

⚓ *RMS* **Lusitania** *was met by a crowd of people at a New York dock in 1907.*

Cunard Line

The Cunard Line launched its first ships in 1840, and for decades, it provided transatlantic service using wooden paddle steamships. Samuel Cunard, the founder of the Cunard Line, modernized the ships in 1878 due in part to increased competition from other shipping companies. From that time on, the Cunard Line developed new models, using technology such as the steam turbine to increase the speed of their passage. The maiden voyages of the *Lusitania* and the *Mauretania* in 1907 set new records for the fastest transatlantic passage, raising the stakes for competing companies. During World War I (1914–1918), half of the Cunard Line ships commandeered by the British Navy were lost in battle, including the *Lusitania*, but the company recovered, and in 1934, it bought out the White Star Line.[4]

Their passengers included inventor Thomas Edison and writer Henry James, who compared the *Mauretania* to a "gentle giantess" that could stride across the entire ocean in a single step.[3]

The White Star Line, now financed by Morgan though still considered a British company, chose to respond by building a new model of steamship. It was impossible to build a ship that was both faster and larger than the *Lusitania* and the *Mauretania*, so the company settled on size over speed. A larger ship would

allow more space for cargo and steerage passengers, as well as opulent accommodations for first-class passengers. The company would make money by booking more emigrant passengers on cheap tickets and by charging more for deluxe first-class tickets. Massive size and luxury, the White Star Line believed, would make this new model of ship competitive.

A New Luxury Liner

The White Star Line developed a plan to build a fleet of sister ships: the *Olympic*, the *Titanic*, and a third ship that was later named *Britannic*. These ocean liners, aside from their record-breaking size, would feature the latest technology, and the design of their first-class suites would mimic luxury hotels. The company planned to spend as much money as necessary on the most reliable engineering and the best building materials. The ships' measurements would surpass the Cunard Line's latest model at 100 feet (30 m) longer and 15,000 short tons (13,600 metric tons) heavier.[5] The only problem was that, at such a massive scale, there were no shipyards equipped to build them. How would these new ships be constructed?

The Olympic

The *Olympic* was built side by side with its sister ship the *Titanic*. Construction started first on the *Olympic*, and it was finished and launched one year earlier than the *Titanic*. It was the only time in history that two ships of such great size were constructed simultaneously at the Harland and Wolff Shipyard in Belfast, Northern Ireland. The ship's maiden voyage from Southampton, England, to New York began on June 14, 1911, and was successfully captained by Edward Smith, who later became the captain of the *Titanic*. The *Olympic* was almost identical to the *Titanic*, with a very similar design and technical capabilities, and it sailed for 24 years before it was retired in 1935.

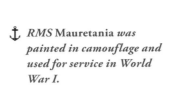

⚓ *RMS* Mauretania *was painted in camouflage and used for service in World War I.*

Chapter 3

BUILDING THE *TITANIC*

T he ships that inspired the *Titanic*, the Cunard Line's *Lusitania* and *Mauretania*, represented more than just technological dominance. The rivalry between the White Star Line and the Cunard Line deepened into an international economic competition. The British government, worried J. P. Morgan's control of the White Star Line would lead to an American shipping monopoly, gave the British-owned Cunard Line huge loans to support the construction of these larger, faster ships.

Bruce Ismay

The chairman of the White Star Line, Bruce Ismay, was the son of the company's founder, Thomas Ismay. He was raised to inherit the company, and his education included an apprenticeship and time spent working at the company's New York office. He married in New York and had four children with his wife, Julia Florence Schieffelin. After his father died, Ismay was persuaded through negotiations to have the White Star Line join Morgan's shipping conglomerate. This deal ultimately led to Ismay losing sole control of the company, but it did not affect the White Star Line's long-standing partnership with shipbuilders Harland and Wolff, who built the *Titanic*. Ismay was on board the *Titanic* during the ship's maiden voyage. Although he survived the sinking, his personal reputation was ruined.

Although the White Star Line didn't have the backing of a wealthy government, Morgan was certainly the next best financier. Morgan, a rich American banker who invested in many industries, provided the money for the White Star Line to build its sister ships—first the *Olympic* and then the *Titanic*. The British chairman of the White Star Line, Bruce Ismay, oversaw the design process, and the chairman of shipbuilders Harland and Wolff, Lord William Pirrie, oversaw the construction. This combination of American money and British technology was a significant shift in the balance of international industry.

Preparation

Harland and Wolff's chief naval architect, Thomas Andrews, worked on the design of the *Titanic*. It was the first ship for which he was fully responsible for the design. His uncle, Alexander Carlisle, the former

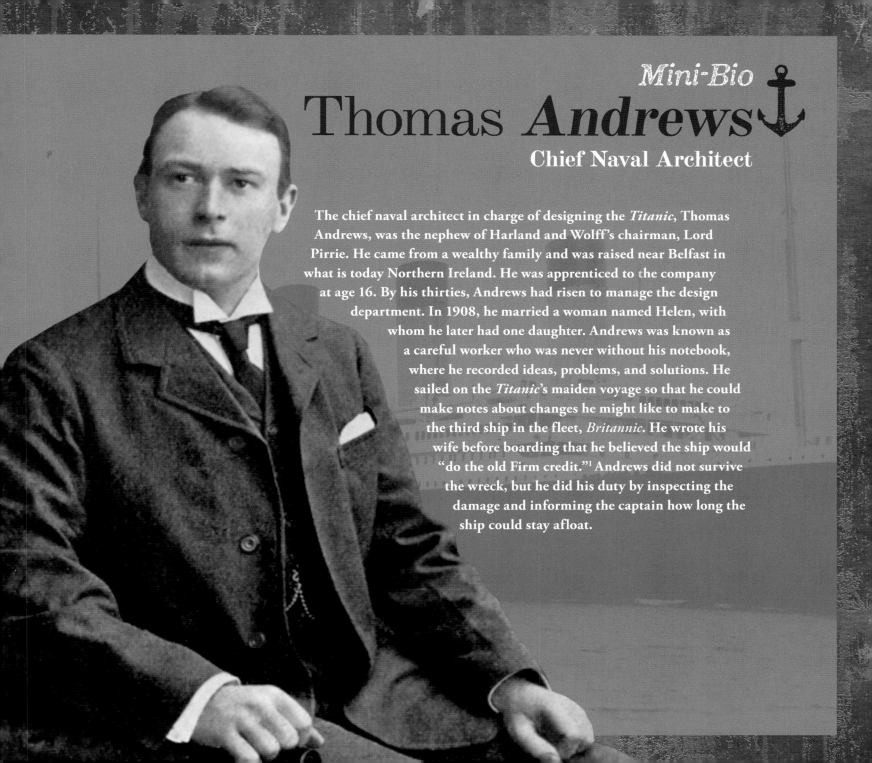

Thomas *Andrews*

Chief Naval Architect

The chief naval architect in charge of designing the *Titanic*, Thomas Andrews, was the nephew of Harland and Wolff's chairman, Lord Pirrie. He came from a wealthy family and was raised near Belfast in what is today Northern Ireland. He was apprenticed to the company at age 16. By his thirties, Andrews had risen to manage the design department. In 1908, he married a woman named Helen, with whom he later had one daughter. Andrews was known as a careful worker who was never without his notebook, where he recorded ideas, problems, and solutions. He sailed on the *Titanic*'s maiden voyage so that he could make notes about changes he might like to make to the third ship in the fleet, *Britannic*. He wrote his wife before boarding that he believed the ship would "do the old Firm credit."[1] Andrews did not survive the wreck, but he did his duty by inspecting the damage and informing the captain how long the ship could stay afloat.

chief naval architect, retired after designing the *Olympic*, and Andrews adapted the design of the *Olympic* for its sister ships. He took no particular risks in the *Titanic*'s design. He was a competent and conscientious architect who had worked on many ships, and he felt confident in his work on the *Titanic*.

Construction of the *Olympic* began at the Harland and Wolff shipyard in Belfast, in what is today Northern Ireland, in December 1908. The yard's new gantry was the largest ever built, and it towered over the slipways where the ships would be constructed. The slipways, gently sloping concrete ramps that allowed the keel, frame, and hull of the ships to be built near the water, were newly built as well.

Because the company planned to build the *Olympic* and the *Titanic* side by side and to accommodate ships of that size, the new gantry was necessary. In order to lift the heavy pieces of steel used in construction, a gantry had to be taller than the completed ship. The *Titanic*'s gantry was 228 feet (69 m) tall—the size of a 22-story building.[2] It was unlike anything the shipbuilders had ever seen before.

The Shipbuilders

Belfast Harbor in March 1909, when the *Titanic*'s construction began, was a hive of activity. Shipbuilding was a major industry in the city, and thousands of shipbuilders worked at the

Harland and Wolff shipyard. Their workday began early, at 6:00 a.m., and stretched until 5:30 p.m., including two breaks for meals. Their workweek ran through Saturday morning, with only a day and a half for their weekend. For those who rose to the rank of foreman, shipbuilding became their entire life. They lived at the shipyard in small cabins to supervise the site.

Shipbuilding was a dangerous job, especially on a project as big as the *Titanic*. Workers' tasks ranged from stoking the heaters and handling red-hot rivets to welding with sparking torches and sledgehammering steel plates. Injuries and even deaths due to the unsafe working conditions were not uncommon. During the construction of the *Titanic*, eight workers died, most from injuries related to falling off the ship's scaffolding.[3] The first death was 15-year-old Sam Scott, who suffered a skull fracture and died instantly.

Worker deaths were an expected part of the shipbuilding process for companies such as Harland and Wolff. Their financial calculations grimly factored

Shipyard Myths

Several myths surround the construction of the *Titanic*, including a story that Catholic shipyard workers sabotaged the ship. There is no evidence that anything like this occurred, although there were tensions between Catholic and Protestant people in Belfast at the time. Another story claimed that a worker was accidentally sealed inside the hull of the ship and died there. Although workers did die during the construction of the *Titanic*, there is no record of anyone dying in that way.

Was the Titanic Really Considered Unsinkable?

Bruce Ismay, chairman of the White Star Line, described the *Titanic* as "practically unsinkable," and most people at the time seemed to believe it.[7] The *Titanic*'s captain, Edward Smith, noted that with advances in shipbuilding technology, "I cannot conceive of any vital disaster happening to this vessel. Modern shipbuilding has gone beyond that."[8] One of these advances, the development of watertight bulkheads, was so trusted that the *Titanic*'s architect, Thomas Andrews, told fellow passengers the ship could be cut into three pieces and still remain afloat. This was true in theory—once the ship's bulkhead doors were closed, each piece would be watertight—but the damage caused by the iceberg collision surpassed expectations.

in one fatality per £100,000 spent on a ship.[4] Based on this calculation, the *Titanic*'s price tag would have allowed for up to 15 worker deaths.[5]

Construction

The main skeleton of the *Titanic* was constructed on the slipway. The first plate of the *Titanic*'s keel was laid on March 31, 1909. During construction, the keel functioned as the backbone of the ship, supporting its massive frame. The frame, the second part of the ship to be built, functioned as a giant ribcage. It was made of curved steel beams that attached to the keel and soared upward, creating a framework in the shape of the ship's hull. The watertight hull, made of huge overlapping steel plates, was constructed over the frame like a skin.

The steel plating of the *Titanic* was high-quality for the time. It was considered "battleship quality" and was made using precise measurements of size and strength.[6]

Each plate, weighing 2 to 3 short tons (1.8 to 2.7 metric tons), was lifted using the gantry and then attached to the ship's frame using the latest hydraulic riveting technology.[9] The bottom of the ship, from the keel to a height of 7 feet (2.1 m), featured a double layer of steel plates for safety.[10]

A Question of Quality

When it was finished, the *Titanic*'s hull contained more than three million rivets through its one-inch- (2.5 cm) thick steel plating.[11] The techniques used to build the *Titanic* were not considered cutting-edge at the time. In fact, the ship's design was fairly conservative. It was based on scaled-up calculations of previous White Star Line ships.

Today, some historians and scientists question whether the hull was strong enough. They wonder if the brittleness of the steel could have caused the hull to crack or the rivets to pop off during the collision with the iceberg. However, engineers who studied the hull's steel plates and rivets have concluded that they were standard for the time and did not contribute to the sinking of the *Titanic*. The *Olympic*, made with the same materials, was a sturdy ship that survived many collisions. In addition, given the speed the *Titanic* was traveling at the time of its collision with the iceberg, even a modern ship would have sustained hull damage. The *Titanic* may have had design errors, but none were markedly different from other ships of its time.

At the time the *Titanic* was launched, it was the largest ship in the world, and its scale gave it the impression of absolute safety. On May 31, 1911, two years and two months after the keel was laid, thousands of people watched as the *Titanic* was launched into Belfast Harbor. The ship was not finished—it had yet to be fitted out with its engines and interiors—but the greatest part of the labor was done.

The *Titanic* would be floated into a fitting-out basin. There, it would be dry-docked while the ship's fittings were installed, from the engine machinery all the way up to the first-class chandeliers.

Watertight Bulkheads

Perhaps the most significant features of the *Titanic*'s design were its watertight bulkheads. The bulkheads divided the ship's hull into 16 separate compartments, allowing the crew to contain a potential leak by closing a series of watertight doors. The ship could remain afloat with up to four compartments flooded. However, this innovative idea could not keep the *Titanic* afloat when more than four compartments flooded, as was the case when it sank.

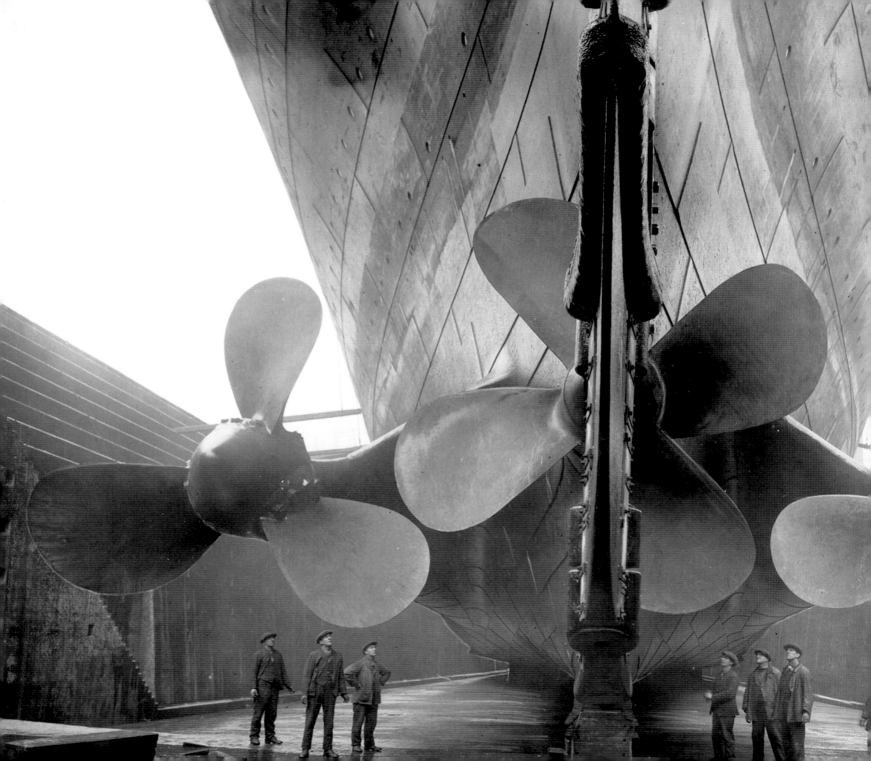

Chapter 4

INSIDE THE
TITANIC

L aunching the *Titanic* was no small endeavor. On the morning of the launch, the slipway where the ship rested was coated with 23 short tons (21 metric tons) of grease, oil, and soap to help ease the ship into the water.[1] As the ship began to move, its own weight and momentum helped pull it down the ramp, and within one minute, the *Titanic* was afloat for the first time.

Fitting Out the Titanic

Once the *Titanic* was docked in the shipyard's fitting-out basin, it was ready to be finished with its machinery and interiors. Despite the steel beams that crisscrossed the inside of the ship marking out the divisions between decks and rooms, it was still essentially an empty hull. From the bottom to the top, everything necessary to the ship's function had to be installed by workers in the coming months.

The most important parts of the ship, the machinery to power it, were installed on the bottom deck, inside the watertight compartments. When the ship was at sea, this deck sat below the waterline so the boilers and engines could drive the propellers outside the ship. Twenty-nine boilers full of water were heated by coal-burning furnaces in order to produce enough steam to power three steam engines the size of large houses.[2] The engines, two traditional engines with pistons and one modern rotating-style turbine engine, each powered one propeller. The propellers were mounted on the ship's stern, one on each side and one in the center. They could push the *Titanic* across the ocean at speeds up to 23 knots, or 26 miles per hour (42 kmh).[3]

Titanic *by the Numbers*

The *Titanic* was a massive ship by almost any standard of its time. The ocean liner had nine decks, most of which were served by four state-of-the-art electric elevators. With 800 cabins and 40 dormitory-style sleeping areas, the ship could carry up to 3,547 passengers and crew. The one-inch- (2.5 cm) thick steel hull was studded with 3 million rivets and 2,000 portholes. Belowdecks, 162 furnaces burned 825 short tons (748 metric tons) of coal per day. These furnaces heated 14,000 gallons (53,000 L) of water per day in 29 boilers, producing enough steam to power the ship's engines.[4]

To steer the ship, workers installed a huge cast-steel rudder behind the propellers. It was a long, thin, curved shape and, as a journalist at the time described, it was "as big as a giant elm tree."[5] The rudder was the same model as the *Olympic*'s, and its efficiency was increased due to its position directly behind the central propeller. The ship could use the propeller's wake in the water to maneuver more effectively.

The ship's smokestacks, known as ventilation funnels, were designed to impress. Four huge funnels rose from the top deck in a straight line from bow to stern, but only three of them were actually functional. The fourth funnel was added for decoration because the White Star Line's designers thought the ship looked more majestic with four. In a few photographs of the *Titanic* at sea, it's possible to see that the fourth funnel did not emit any smoke, but in other photos, the White Star Line had smoke drawn in to complete the illusion.

Sea Trials

Before the *Titanic* could begin its maiden voyage, the ship was required to pass sea trials. Sea trials were conducted by the British Board of Trade and consisted of several tests to determine a ship's seaworthiness. Officials observed and recorded a ship's speed, maneuverability, and stopping capability, among other markers of readiness to sail. Although ships were generally not pushed to perform at their very best during sea trials, these measurements were the only hard evidence of the *Titanic*'s capabilities. During sea trials the *Titanic* demonstrated speeds of up to 20 knots, or 23 miles per hour (37 kmh), a turning radius of 3,850 yards (3,520 m), and a stopping distance of 850 yards (777 m).[6] These results compared well with other ships of the time.

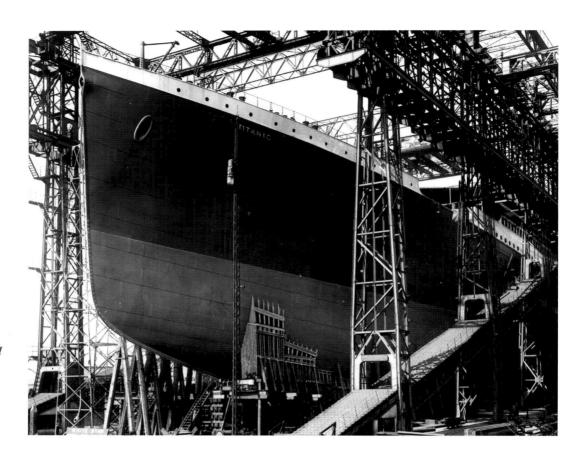

Inside the cabins on the upper decks, workers installed all the fittings that could be desired by the wealthy first-class passengers, as well as by the growing market of middle-class passengers traveling in second class. Wiring for electric lights and plumbing for running water were connected across the ship, and the final details were installed just before the *Titanic* was due to sail in March 1912, although the launch was delayed to early April 1912.

Belfast to Southampton

The distance from Belfast, Northern Ireland, to the port of Southampton, England, where the *Titanic* would begin its maiden voyage, was approximately 500 miles (800 km). The ship set out from Belfast Harbor on April 2 with a small crew, White Star Line officials, and representatives of the Board of Trade.[7] The crew spent one day completing the necessary sea trials to test the ship's seaworthiness and then sailed through the Irish Sea toward the southern coast of England.

The port of Southampton was a bustling town not very far from the city of London. Ships docked there often in preparation for their maiden voyages, as the *Titanic* did. It was an easy place to recruit sailors, as many of them lived there, and to purchase supplies for the passage across the Atlantic Ocean. The *Titanic* spent six days in port while its new crew was hired on.

Titanic's Crew

The crew necessary to staff the *Titanic* for its maiden voyage was approximately 900 people.[8] From the top deck, where the captain and officers worked, through the passengers' quarters, where the stewards and stewardesses served, to the bottom deck where the stokers and engineers labored, the ship was full of employees. It was as much a workplace as it was a luxury ship.

Mini-Bio
Edward *Smith*
Captain

Edward Smith was a high-ranking captain of the White Star Line, and he commanded the company's newest ships on their maiden voyages. In 1911, he sailed the *Olympic*, *Titanic*'s sister ship, on its successful passage to New York. Smith was a favorite captain of many wealthy passengers, who found him intelligent, friendly, and a good storyteller. The son of a shopkeeper, Smith left home at the age of 13 when he was apprenticed to a shipping company. He worked for the White Star Line for 30 years, commanded troop ships during Britain's Boer War (1899–1902), and was well liked by the officers who served under him. Smith, with his wife, Eleanor, and daughter, Helen, settled in the port town of Southampton. A tall man with a neatly trimmed white beard, Smith cut quite a figure as a captain, and after his death on the *Titanic*, a wax statue of him was featured at London's Madame Tussauds Exhibition.

Captain Smith and his six officers had personal quarters near the ship's bridge, the area where navigation took place. The bridge included a room where the officers charted their course and a wheelhouse where they supervised the sailors steering their course. The ship's officers commanded the deck crew. Sailors known as quartermasters did the actual steering in the wheelhouse, while the lookouts manned the crow's nest directly ahead of the bridge. The ship's boatswain supervised the sailors who carried out the daily work of maintaining the ship.

Belowdecks, a different hierarchy governed the victualing crew. Victualing referred to the victuals, or food, this crew managed, along with supplies and passenger services. The purser, who managed the money on board, oversaw this crew. The kitchen staff worked in the multiple kitchens used to prepare food for the passengers, depending on their class. Approximately 300 stewards and 20 stewardesses cleaned rooms, delivered items, and saw to passengers' needs.

On the bottom deck, the engine crew kept the ship running day and night. Engineers and electricians maintained and repaired the ship's machinery, while stokers and trimmers shoveled coal for the furnaces. Nearly 300 stokers and trimmers worked shifts in the hot boiler rooms and dusty coal bunkers. They spent all of their time on the lower decks of the ship. The first- and second-class passengers were likely unaware how large the crew really was. On the *Titanic*'s maiden voyage, there were approximately seven crew members for every ten guests.

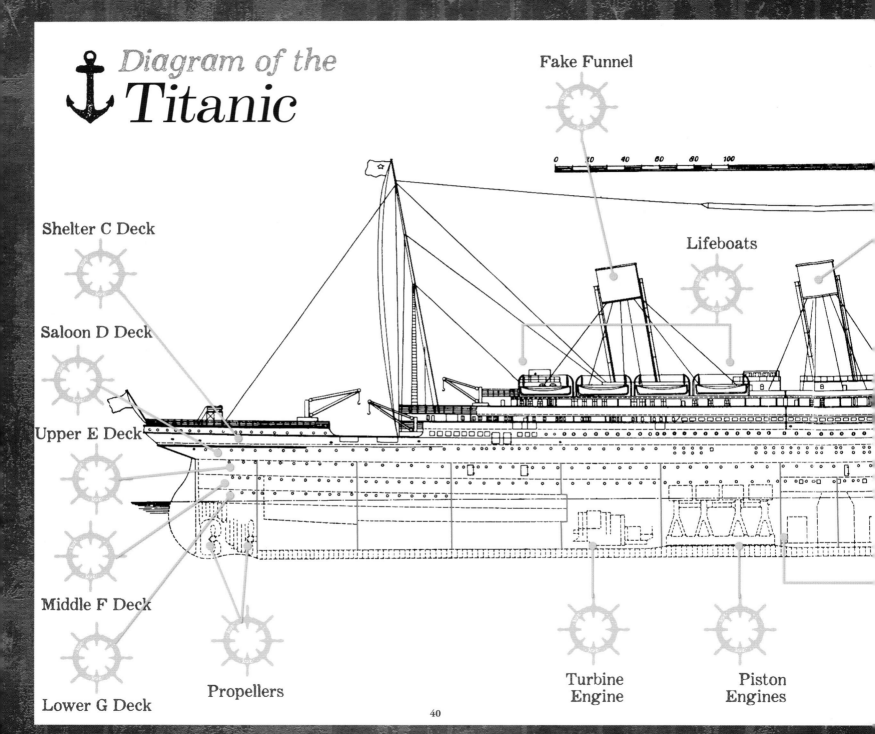

Diagram of the Titanic

Fake Funnel

Shelter C Deck

Saloon D Deck

Upper E Deck

Middle F Deck

Lower G Deck

Propellers

Lifeboats

Turbine Engine

Piston Engines

0   20   40   60   80   100

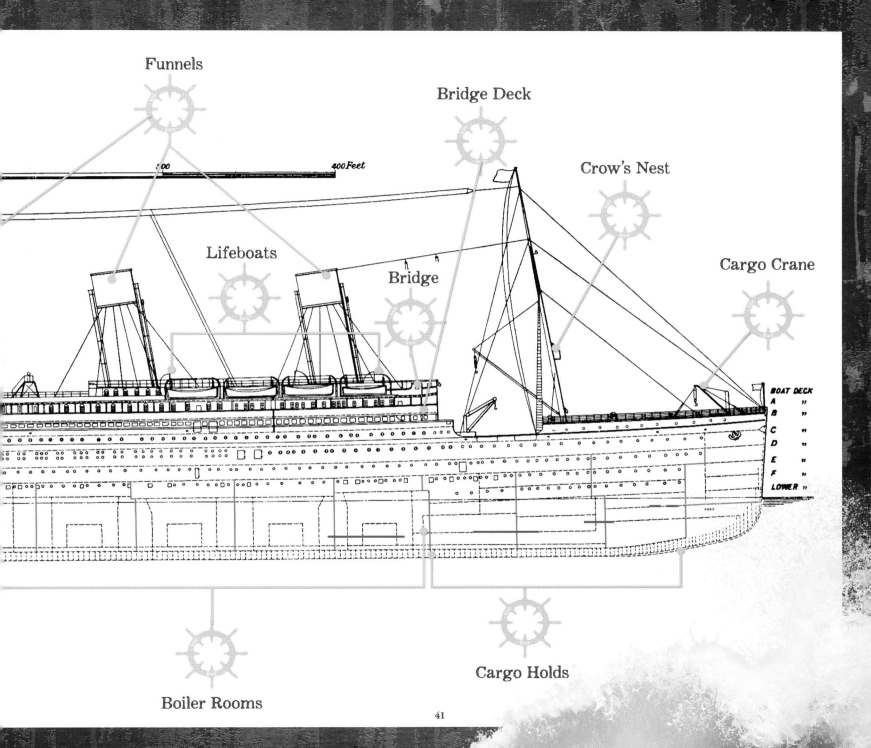

Funnels

Bridge Deck

Crow's Nest

Cargo Crane

400 Feet

Lifeboats

Bridge

BOAT DECK
A "
B "
C "
D "
E "
F "
LOWER "

Cargo Holds

Boiler Rooms

41

Chapter 5

BON VOYAGE

The *Titanic* left Southampton at noon on April 10, 1912, and its maiden voyage was finally under way. The ship had been in port for six days, with officers hiring and training crew members and workers finishing last-minute interior fittings. Everyone on board was busy preparing the ship for its first journey across the Atlantic Ocean.

All Aboard

The *Titanic* was built to carry 2,566 passengers, and although it was only 51 percent booked for its maiden voyage, the ship was stocked with huge amounts of supplies.[1] In the days leading up to the ship's departure, trainloads full of food and household items were delivered to the docks and loaded onto the ship via crane. Inside the ship,

Victuals

The *Titanic*'s storage rooms were packed full of food for the kitchen staff to prepare during the journey, including:

- ⚓ Bacon and ham: 7,500 pounds (3,400 kg)
- ⚓ Poultry: 25,000 pounds (11,340 kg)
- ⚓ Potatoes: 40 short tons (36 metric tons)
- ⚓ Green peas: 2,500 pounds (1,130 kg)
- ⚓ Cereal: 10,000 pounds (4,540 kg)
- ⚓ Butter: 6,000 pounds (2,720 kg)
- ⚓ Ice cream: 1,750 pounds (790 kg)
- ⚓ Grapefruit: 13,000
- ⚓ Beer: 15,000 bottles[2]

workers painted walls, hauled and arranged furniture, and hung curtains.

On the lower decks of the ship, multiple storage rooms were packed full of thousands of pounds of meat, vegetables, cereal, coffee, alcohol, and more. In the ship's many kitchens, cabinets were stacked high with plates, glasses, teacups, and saltshakers. The stewards' linen closets were fully stocked with sheets, blankets, pillows, and towels. It was a massive undertaking to essentially pack up the equivalent of a hotel at sea.

Commercial cargo arriving by rail for the *Titanic* was loaded using dockside cranes. Mounted on rails, the cranes moved between the railroad cars and the ship, swiveling and lifting the bulky boxes of cargo. The businesses shipping cargo to New York included several companies that still exist today, such as Wells Fargo, American Express, and Tiffany & Co. The ship's cargo holds were loaded with nearly $500,000 worth of products, from automobiles to ostrich feathers.[3]

Passengers began arriving at the dock in Southampton on the morning of April 10. Some had traveled to Southampton the day prior and spent the night at one of the many hotels or inns near the port. Other passengers arrived on trains that the White Star Line had chartered from London. The trains delivered passengers directly to the docks and were scheduled based on ticket class. Second- and third-class passenger trains left London early and arrived in Southampton at 9:30 a.m. First-class passengers had more time to make their train, as it left London two hours later and arrived in Southampton just one half hour before the *Titanic* was due to depart.

As the time drew nearer to noon, the docks began to fill with onlookers eager to see off the world's largest ship. The scene was chaotic as porters hurried late passengers and their luggage

Cargo

The *Titanic* transported cargo for British businesses, including products intended for sale in the United States, including:

- 34 cases of athletic goods
- 8 cases of orchids
- 1 case of Edison gramophones
- 856 rolls of linoleum
- 15 cases of rabbit hair
- 4 cases of opium[4]

Why Were the Titanic's Passengers Traveling?

Most of the *Titanic*'s passengers traveling in third class were immigrants moving to the United States. The first-class passengers were largely vacationers. Second class included some immigrants, as well as passengers on business trips or visiting family. Several couples on board were newlyweds celebrating their honeymoons. But one of the most fascinating passenger stories belongs to the Navratil brothers, two young boys whose father had kidnapped them from their mother in France. Under an assumed name, he brought them on board the *Titanic* and planned to start a new life in the United States. He did not survive the shipwreck, but as the ship was about to sink, he placed the boys in a lifeboat. One month after the wreck, their mother recognized the brothers from pictures in a newspaper and came to New York, where she was reunited with her sons.

⚓ *The* Titanic *was only about one-half full of its maximum passenger capacity when it set sail on April 10, 1912.*

toward the gangways, while gawkers staring up at the huge ship blocked their way. Parents attempted to keep track of their children, and sailors rushed with their kits along the dockside as the ship's officers signaled for the gangways to be withdrawn. High up on the *Titanic*'s decks, passengers pressed against the railings to wave goodbye and watch as the ship began pulling away from the shore.

Signs of Trouble

It took five tugboats to pull the *Titanic* out of port, and the operation was a delicate one. Several other ships were moored along the docks, and the *Titanic* had to be maneuvered past them safely. The crowd sending the ship off ran alongside to watch, and passengers on other ships waved and craned their necks to get a good look at the spectacle. But one of the other ships, the *New York*, had a very close encounter with the *Titanic*.

As the *Titanic* neared the *New York*, its powerful wake strained the ropes mooring the smaller ship to the dock. With a loud crack, several of the ropes snapped, sending one end of the ship swinging out into the channel. The *New York* came within four feet (1.2 m) of slamming into the side of the *Titanic*. At the *Titanic*'s wheel, the first officer engaged one of the propellers, creating a wave that pushed the smaller ship back. The *New York* drifted away at an angle—directly into the *Titanic*'s path. The *Titanic* nearly plowed into the *New York*, but the huge ship managed to halt just in time. This dramatic scene set the onlookers buzzing, and some passengers worried it was a bad sign for the large ocean liner.

The passengers did not know that eight decks below, the *Titanic* had a potentially more serious problem. For days before the *Titanic* left port, there had been a fire smoldering in one of the coal bunkers. Because the storage area was full of coal, the fire slowly fed itself, and it proved impossible for the workers to put it out entirely. It wasn't

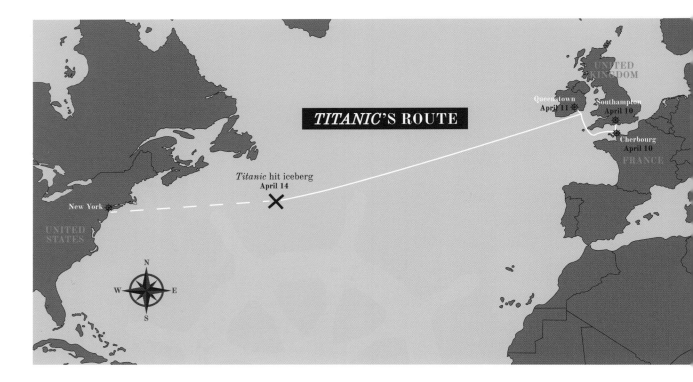

⚓ *The* **Titanic's** *last stop was Queenstown, Ireland.*

until several days after the ship was out to sea, when most of the coal in the bunker had been fed into the boiler furnaces, that workers were able to smother the fire.

The Journey Begins

As the *Titanic* left Southampton behind and entered deep water, the first officer engaged the propellers and set a course. Due to the near collision with the *New York*, the ship was running behind schedule for its first stop—Cherbourg, France. Crossing the English Channel went smoothly, and by the time the *Titanic* dropped anchor off the coast of France, twilight was beginning to settle over the water.

The port of Cherbourg was too small for the *Titanic* to sail into. The 22 disembarking passengers were brought to shore in a boat, while the 274 boarding passengers were ferried out to the ship.[5] Among the many first-class passengers boarding in Cherbourg were the wealthiest guests on the *Titanic*, American millionaire J. J. Astor and his young wife, Madeleine, who were returning home from their honeymoon.

From France, the *Titanic* turned toward Ireland, where the ship would make its last stop before heading out into the ocean. Queenstown, on Ireland's southern coast, was also too small a port for the *Titanic*, which anchored two miles (3.2 km) offshore. Seven passengers disembarked from the ship, and 120 passengers boarded.[6] Most of them were emigrants with third-class tickets. Finally, after hundreds of bags of mail bound for New York were loaded on board, the *Titanic*'s great engines fired up again, and the ship steamed ahead, gathering speed.

Last Man Off

Likely the last person to disembark from the *Titanic* before its final journey, James Coffey deserted the ship's crew in Queenstown, Ireland. The 23-year-old stoker joined the crew in Southampton and worked in the boiler rooms for the first two days of the ship's passage before abandoning his position at the last European stop. Queenstown was Coffey's hometown, but he spent little time there after deserting the *Titanic*. Within a week he had signed on to another ship's crew and left port.

⚓ *Much of the Titanic was designed with luxury and style in mind, including the staircase. A replica is featured as a private event space at Titanic Belfast, a tourist attraction at the former site of the Harland and Wolff Shipyard in Belfast, Northern Ireland.*

Chapter 6

ON THE OPEN OCEAN

As the *Titanic* left Europe behind, passengers began settling into daily life on the ship. They expected to arrive in New York within one week of departing Southampton, and until then, there was little to do except enjoy the trip. For passengers in first class, there were plenty of luxuries to explore. For many passengers in second or third class, the experience of being on an ocean liner was new and exciting in itself.

What Was the Marconi Wireless?

Invented by Guglielmo Marconi, the wireless message, also known as the telegram, became popular in the early 1900s. Before radio waves carried music or news into people's homes, Marconi wireless stations used radio waves to send messages to other stations over both land and water. This technology was important for navigation at sea because for the first time ships that were not within eyeshot of each other could communicate. Wireless operators on ships could send messages up to a range of 500 miles (800 km).[3] Operators were young male radio enthusiasts employed by Marconi's company, and on the *Titanic* they played a significant role in the events leading up to and following the iceberg collision. Without wireless technology, rescue would have taken longer and fewer people would have survived the shipwreck.

First Class

Almost as soon as the *Titanic* departed, first-class passengers clamored for their personal messages to be sent over the ship's wireless system. The Marconi wireless, a new technology that used Morse code to transmit messages, was the fastest way to communicate. However, the price to send a wireless message made it a luxury. For just the first ten words, the cost was 12 shillings and sixpence, which today would be approximately $62.[1] Even with that high price, the *Titanic*'s wireless operators sent and received more than 250 messages for passengers.[2]

The wealthy people who traveled in first class were accustomed to amenities, but the *Titanic* was extravagant even by their standards. The ship offered a heated swimming pool—the first ever on an ocean liner—and Turkish baths, a trend at the time that was similar to a sauna. One woman who tried the

Turkish baths could not bear the extreme heat, however. She wrote in her journal, "I never disliked anything in my life so before, though I enjoyed the final plunge in the pool."[4] Other adventurous passengers could try out the mechanical camel in the ship's gym, a piece of exercise equipment that simulated the experience of riding a camel.

In 1912, society was often segregated by gender, and there were areas of the *Titanic* reserved for men, such as the barbershop and the smoking room. Here, many businessmen lounged and discussed their work. Others spent their time playing poker, drinking, and sizing each other up according to wealth and social status.

Many of the women in first class gathered at the Palm Court or the Café Parisien to socialize. Some walked along the deck promenades greeting each other and gossiping. Others spent time in their suites, enjoying private parlors, marble fireplaces, and the ability to telephone a stewardess for anything they required. In the evenings, there were multicourse

Titanic's *Orchestra*

The *Titanic* employed eight musicians who performed each evening as one quintet and one trio. The quintet was led by English violinist Wallace Hartley, and the trio was led by French violinist Georges Krins. Musicians on White Star Line ships were required to memorize more than 350 songs that passengers might request, so their work was more complicated than playing a set list. All the musicians traveled in second class, and their ages ranged from 20 to 40 years old. On the night of the collision, the musicians came together and played as a single orchestra to help comfort the passengers while the ship sank. None of them survived, and only three of their bodies were ever found.

Margaret Brown

First-Class Passenger

Known to many people today as "the unsinkable Molly Brown," a name she never actually used, Margaret Brown was a first-class passenger on the *Titanic*. A formerly working-class millionaire whose husband had struck gold in a Colorado mine, Brown had held a job in a tobacco factory from age 13 to 18. She was confident and intelligent—she spoke four languages—and had a good sense of humor, which helped her navigate wealthy society. Brown had been traveling in Europe after separating from her husband and was returning home when the *Titanic* sank. By the time the ship that rescued survivors reached New York, Brown had rallied first-class passengers to donate thousands of dollars to those who had lost everything in the wreck. She gained notoriety by telling reporters, "The ship can sink, but I can't; I'm unsinkable!"[5]

dinners offered at several restaurants, as well as dancing and piano and orchestra concerts. For those traveling in first class, the *Titanic* had "everything but taxi-cabs and theatres," one passenger remarked.[6]

Second Class

For passengers traveling in second class, such as Charlotte Collyer and her family, the *Titanic*'s accommodations were still extremely impressive. The second-class rooms on the ship were very similar to first-class rooms on smaller ocean liners. As Harvey Collyer put it, everything was "swank."[7] The family's room featured a mahogany bunkbed, a sofa, and electric heating and lighting. For many middle-class passengers, whose jobs ranged from ministers to shopkeepers, these were luxuries. To one young passenger, an apprentice butcher, the *Titanic* seemed to be "a floating palace."[8]

The public rooms in second class were large, comfortable, and in their basics similar to first class. The lounge offered a library of books and several writing and card tables, while the smoking room was the place for men to play poker and drink. Men also gathered in the barbershop, where, besides a shave and haircut, they could buy trinkets and memorabilia. Children typically played outside on the boat deck, overseen by mothers who were talking among themselves or reading novels on the folding deck chairs. Games such as shuffleboard

Titanic's Menu

The last full meal served on the *Titanic* was Sunday dinner on April 14. As usual, three different menus were prepared.

FIRST CLASS

Oysters, cream of barley soup, salmon with mousseline sauce, roast duckling with apple sauce, sirloin of beef, chateau potatoes, cold asparagus, pâté de foie gras, peaches in Chartreuse jelly, chocolate and vanilla éclairs, and ice cream

SECOND CLASS

Consommé, baked haddock with sharp sauce, curried chicken and rice, lamb with mint sauce, roast turkey with cranberry sauce, green peas, roast potatoes, plum pudding, and ice cream

THIRD CLASS

Rice soup, fresh bread, biscuits, roast beef with gravy, sweet corn, boiled potatoes, and plum pudding with sweet sauce

⚓ *Visitors to Titanic Belfast in Belfast, Northern Ireland, can see replicas of the* Titanic's *third-class cabins.*

and ring toss were popular, as well as chess or checkers, which were played inside the lounge.

Though second-class passengers had only one dining room, their meals were elegant and featured several courses. Diners listened to live piano music played by other passengers while they ate, and the children could swivel back and forth in the red leather upholstered chairs, which were bolted to the floor in case of rough seas. After dinner, it was common for men to gather in the smoking room while women and children socialized in the lounge.

Third Class

The steerage accommodations on the *Titanic* were better than those on most ocean liners, but there was a distinct separation between second- and third-class passengers. Most passengers traveling in steerage were emigrants who had very little money. From skilled tradesmen, such

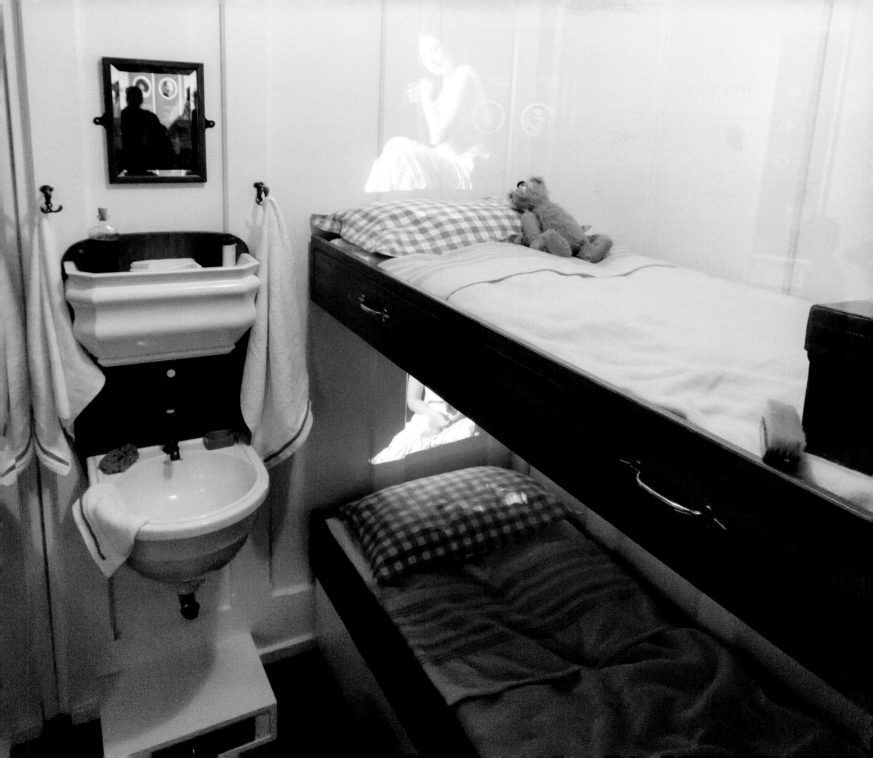

as blacksmiths and shoemakers, to farmers, laborers, and servants, some third-class passengers carried everything they owned along with them.

Steerage cabins were dormitory-style, most with four to six bunks per room. Families could have a private room, but single passengers often shared their room with several strangers, men in the bow of the ship and women in the stern. All cabins had electric heat and light, as well as sinks with running water, though bathrooms were shared. Third class was located on the ship's lower decks, near the engines and boiler rooms, and it could be noisy. For some children, however, being able to sneak in and watch the engine crew work was the best entertainment on board.

Social life in third class was mostly self-made. The amenities were limited to a men's smoking room and a large public lounge with wooden benches where all third-class passengers could gather. Access to the ship's rear deck allowed adults to walk in the fresh air and children to play games and jump rope. Passengers played music in the evenings, singing and dancing together. Many emigrants, particularly those who did not speak English, traveled in groups, and those who were emigrating alone usually made friends with others who spoke their native language. There were passengers of many ethnicities on board, including Irish, Swedish, Lebanese, Chinese, Greek, Russian Jewish, and Armenian. Most of them had never seen an ocean liner like the *Titanic* before in their lives or taken such a long vacation from daily work.

Jamilah Nīqūla *Yārid* ⚓

Lebanese Emigrant

A teenage Lebanese emigrant, Jamilah Nīqūla Yārid traveled on the *Titanic* in third class. Although she was just 14 years old and spoke no English, she and her 11-year-old brother, Ilyās, were alone on the journey. They had left their hometown in the mountains with their father, a flour miller, and sailed from Beirut to Marseilles, France. There, during an immigration medical check, the doctor diagnosed their father with a contagious eye infection, and he was not allowed to continue on their journey. Traveling alone, Jamilah and Ilyās boarded the *Titanic* at Cherbourg, planning to meet their older brother in New York. Their father would follow later. Ultimately, their father's setback was lucky. Jamilah and Ilyās, as children, were saved from the shipwreck, but their father would likely have died. Instead, the family was eventually reunited in the United States, where they settled in Florida.

⚓ *Beirut at the turn of the twentieth century*

⚓ *First-class guests enjoyed spending time on the promenade deck of the* **Titanic.**

Chapter 7

ICEBERG AHEAD

The morning of Sunday, April 14, dawned clear and calm on the North Atlantic Ocean, and many passengers on the *Titanic* readied themselves for church services. Clergy on board offered Catholic mass and Church of England services. While passengers were at prayer, the ship sailed on, closer to the icy cold ocean currents near Newfoundland, and the air temperature began to drop.

Sunday Afternoon

The chilly afternoon discouraged most passengers from enjoying the fresh air on the ship's decks, though some did bundle up in heavy coats and scarves for a short walk. To keep warm and pass the time, third-class passengers held a dance in their lounge, with music from accordions, harmonicas, and fiddles. Off-duty crew joined in from time to time, while men who preferred not to dance played cards in the smoking room. Several decks above, men in second and first class enjoyed the same activity, while mothers watched their children run and play on an enclosed promenade deck. As the afternoon grew colder, several women retired to their cabins and turned on the electric heaters for some relief.

Inside the Marconi room on the ship's bridge, the wireless operators tapped out messages at a feverish pace. Jack Phillips and Harold Bride had worked the entire trip to keep up with passengers' demand for wireless messages, and although they both loved the technology, it was an exhausting task. Their wireless set had broken the previous evening, and both men worked overnight to repair it. They had to pull a double shift to catch up on the ship's communications.

Fred Fleet

The lookout who first spotted the iceberg that sank the *Titanic*, Fred Fleet, had been a sailor for nine years. He signed onto the *Titanic*'s crew at age 24 with four years' experience working on another ship. From Liverpool, England, originally, Fleet had never known his father and was abandoned at a young age by his mother. He was raised in a series of orphanages and foster families until age 12, when he entered training to become a sailor. On the night of the shipwreck, Fleet remained on duty in the crow's nest until he was assigned to help with loading the lifeboats. He survived the sinking and sailed for many more years, but he never seemed to recover from the trauma of the *Titanic* disaster. Homeless and penniless at age 77, he took his own life.

⚓ *Marconi wireless machines were used to transmit messages using Morse code.*

In addition to passenger messages, the operators often received wireless communications from other ships in the area. Earlier in the day, they delivered a message to Captain Smith from the crew of a steamship advising that they had spotted icebergs. A similar message was delivered in the afternoon. A third such message came through but was not passed on to the captain because it was addressed to the Hydrographic Office in Washington, DC. By evening, a fourth iceberg message was delivered to the bridge, while a fifth message was delayed because of the backlog of passenger messages Phillips and Bride were busy relaying. It was this last message that might have made a difference in the *Titanic*'s course, though by the time it was received, the captain and bridge crew were well aware that ships nearby had encountered icebergs.

The Collision

As the sun set and darkness fell around the ship, passengers sat down to Sunday dinner. Captain Smith joined a friend's dinner party, but at nine o'clock in the evening he checked in on the bridge before retiring to his room. The bridge, crewed by several officers, was dark, illuminated only by the green compass light. The first officer, William Murdoch, had asked that all lights at the front of the ship be dimmed so that the lookouts could see beyond the glare to any icebergs that might lie ahead.

Up in the crow's nest, the lookouts had an extremely difficult task. Aside from the freezing temperatures, the night was so still that there were no waves, which usually would act as a visual marker for an iceberg. Without a bright moon to reflect off the ice or waves to lap against the base of it, spotting an object in the dark of night was nearly impossible. Still, as lookout Fred Fleet scanned the horizon, he noticed a haze ahead that slowly resolved into a small object. Within seconds, the object appeared to grow in size as the ship sailed closer. It was an iceberg,

⚓ *William Murdoch was the officer in charge when the* Titanic *struck the iceberg.*

and Fleet reached out to strike the alarm bell. Beside him, his partner kept his eye on the ice while Fleet telephoned the bridge.

"What do you see?" James Moody, the officer in the wheelhouse, asked.

"Iceberg right ahead," Fleet reported and heard Moody hang up swiftly.[1]

Distress Calls in Morse Code

Before Captain Smith left the bridge to investigate the extent of the ship's damage, he spoke to the Marconi wireless operators, Jack Phillips and Harold Bride, and informed them of the collision. When he returned to the bridge one-half hour after the collision, Captain Smith gave the operators the order to begin sending out distress calls. At first, Phillips used the distress call "CQD," which to wireless operators meant "all stations: emergency."[2] It was followed by the ship's name and location. After a few minutes, it occurred to Bride to try the newer distress call "SOS," which was faster to tap out in Morse code.[3] Both distress calls were understood by nearby ships, and the *Titanic* operators used them interchangeably that night.

On the bridge, First Officer Murdoch called for the quartermaster to turn the wheel hard to starboard. Very slowly, the *Titanic*'s bow began to turn. Murdoch ordered the engines to stop and reverse, a maneuver that he believed would swing the ship away from the iceberg.

Fleet watched the dark shape of the iceberg slide along the starboard side of the ship—closer, closer—until a spray of ice showered across the deck below him. It seemed to him as though the ship grazed the iceberg but avoided a collision.

In fact, the maneuver exposed the side of the *Titanic*, allowing the iceberg to scrape and gouge along the length of the ship underwater. Within one minute of Fleet's sighting of the iceberg, the ship was badly damaged. Turning was a poor miscalculation, and perhaps Murdoch realized it because he quickly reached for the switch to close the ship's watertight bulkhead doors.

Captain Smith, striding onto the bridge, called out, "What have we struck?"

"An iceberg, sir," Murdoch acknowledged.[4]

A Bump in the Night

A sudden jolt woke Jamilah Nīqūla Yārid from sleep in her bunk in steerage. She cried out and clutched at the edge of her bed, cold and frightened in the dark room. Her younger brother, Ilyās, was awake in the bunk beneath hers. "Something's wrong," she called to him urgently.

"Go back to sleep," he complained. "You worry too much!"[5]

Many passengers were not so concerned, though. In another second-class room, Selena Cook lay in bed, glaring at the wall. The boys next door must be pillow fighting again, she thought, irritated.

What Did the Collision Feel Like?

Passenger and crew experiences of the *Titanic*'s collision with the iceberg depended on where they were on the ship.

⚓ "It was just as though we went over about a thousand marbles."[6] –Ella White, first-class passenger

⚓ "It very nearly sent me off my feet."[7] –William Lucas, deck crew

⚓ "An extra heave of the engines and a more than usually obvious dancing motion of the mattress."[8] –Lawrence Beesley, second-class passenger

⚓ "We sort of felt a rip that gave a sort of twist to the whole room."[9] –Hugh Woolner, first-class passenger

⚓ "I heard some terrible noise and I jumped out on the floor, and the first thing I knew my feet were getting wet."[10] –Daniel Buckley, third-class passenger

Over the years, many artists have illustrated what the sinking of the Titanic *may have looked like.*

Chapter 8

DISASTER

Down in boiler room six, a red light came on. The lead stoker called for the dampers to be shut, cutting off the air supply to the furnaces and putting out the coal fire that powered the ship's engines. But just as the engines were beginning to slow, a cascade of freezing water flooded into the boiler room. Then, the door in the watertight bulkhead began to close on the stokers.

In the Boiler Rooms

As the bulkhead door lowered, its heavy steel clanking, the stokers dove for the opening. On the other side in the next watertight compartment, boiler room five was also flooding. There, the stokers could see a rupture in the side of the ship where the rivets had split apart. A rush of seawater sprayed all the way across the floor into the empty coal bunker.

The engine crew went to work. Despite the danger, they labored hard to hold down the water level in boiler room five, pumping it back out as fast as they could. By attaching a wide suction hose made of leather to their pump, they managed to control the flooding for nearly an hour. But as boiler room six next door filled up, the pressure on the bulkhead door became too strong, and a wave of water burst through, driving the crew back.

On the Bridge

Captain Smith had just sent his fourth officer, Joseph Boxhall, to do a damage inspection when the ship's carpenter came running onto the bridge. "The ship is making water," he reported, out of breath.[1] Within ten minutes, Boxhall himself returned with even worse news. The mailroom was flooding so badly that it was certain the deck below it must be underwater. Smith was silent as he took in this information, and then went to inform the wireless operators to stand by in case the *Titanic* needed to send a distress call. First, he wanted to see the damage for himself.

With the ship's architect Thomas Andrews, Smith ventured belowdecks. The men learned that three cargo holds and two boiler rooms had split open as the ship's side scraped past the iceberg. In total, six of the sixteen watertight compartments were taking on seawater, and the

Collision Timeline

⚓ **11:40 p.m.**—Lookout Fred Fleet sights an iceberg and alerts the bridge; First Officer Murdoch orders the ship to turn, but the *Titanic* strikes the iceberg.

⚓ **12:00 a.m.**—Captain Smith learns the ship will sink within a couple of hours.

⚓ **12:05 a.m.**—Captain Smith orders the lifeboats to be prepared for evacuation.

⚓ **12:45 a.m.**—Crew launch the first lifeboat.

⚓ **2:05 a.m.**—Crew launch the last lifeboat.

⚓ **2:20 a.m.**—The *Titanic* sinks.

ship was not built to withstand that volume of flooding. As it continued to fill with water, the bow of the *Titanic* would sink lower and lower into the ocean until its weight pulled the rest of the ship down with it.

Smith and Andrews returned to the bridge, soberly discussing how long it might take for the ship to sink. Andrews calculated that they had at most two hours left afloat. Distress calls needed to be sent out at once. Smith gave orders to prepare and launch the lifeboats, aware that there were not enough of them to save all the passengers. Women and children should be loaded into the boats, he directed. However, he did not direct officers to raise a general alarm throughout the ship.

Who Heard the Titanic's Distress Call?

Several ships heard and answered the *Titanic*'s distress call on the night of the collision, including its sister ship the *Olympic*. The closest ship to answer was the *Carpathia*, approximately 58 miles (93 km) away, which rescued the *Titanic*'s survivors the following morning. The Marconi wireless operator on the *Carpathia*, Harold Cottam, was getting ready for bed when he happened to catch the distress call. He had been waiting for a response from the *Parisian* and kept his headphones on while taking off his coat. As he bent to untie his bootlaces, he heard the *Titanic* call for assistance. After confirming that it was a distress call, he took the message to the captain of the *Carpathia*, who immediately turned the ship and headed toward the *Titanic* at full speed.

The ship's officers, following Smith's orders, assured passengers that loading the lifeboats was just a precaution. They strongly encouraged women and children to board the boats, but told them there was no need to worry. Word of the collision spread, but no official announcement was made, and soon, contradictory messages trickled down through the ship's crew.

To the Lifeboats

Many crew members were completely uninformed of the seriousness of the situation. "Wrap up warmly for you may have a little trip for an hour or so in one of our lifeboats," one first-class passenger's steward advised her.[2] Other crew members knocked on cabin doors and guided passengers to the decks, all the while promising them that there was no danger.

⚓ Titanic's *lifeboats could hold fewer than 1,200 people, and there were more than 2,200 passengers and crew on board.*

On the boat deck, officers hurried to load the lifeboats, calling for women and children. However, the majority of passengers were still belowdecks, unaware that boats were being launched. Of those who were on deck, some women, such as Charlotte Collyer, were reluctant to leave their husbands and the apparent safety of the huge ship.

Why Were Women and Children Evacuated First?

The phrase "women and children first" came from the wreck of HMS *Birkenhead* in 1852, a ship that carried an unusually high number of families on board.[4] It is often considered an unwritten rule of disasters at sea; however a 2012 study by Swedish economists revealed that historically, a ship's crew had a better rate of survival than its passengers. Among passengers, men fared the best, followed by women, and then children. A captain's order was the only factor that increased the survival rate of women and children. As the *Titanic* began to sink, Captain Smith ordered that women and children be loaded into lifeboats. The crew obeyed, though sometimes to tragic effect: Second Officer Herbert Lightoller interpreted Smith's order as "women and children only," and refused to evacuate men at all.[5]

The *Titanic* carried 20 lifeboats, including four collapsible boats.[3] In an effort to launch as many of the lifeboats as possible before the ship sank, most of the boats were not filled to capacity. Several officers were cautious about how many people could safely be lowered in the boats. As a result, if there were no more passengers nearby willing to board a lifeboat, the crew simply launched it half-full and moved on to load the next boat. Crew members were needed to row the lifeboats, and so each boat that was launched left behind fewer crew to manage the evacuation. The lack of a clear plan made the evacuation disorganized and confusing—a recipe for disaster.

By 1:00 a.m., distress signal rockets were fired up over the ship, and passengers began to understand the truth. With the booming, bursting lights in the sky, some men on deck became frantic, and Captain Smith bellowed at them through his megaphone to stay back from the lifeboats. Within 20 minutes, however, a surge of passengers from second and third class reached the boat deck and, taking in the scene, realized that there would not be enough lifeboats to save them all.

With only six boats left and hundreds of passengers on deck, the final hour of the evacuation was daunting. The last two regular lifeboats were launched, as well as two of the collapsible boats. Officers attempted to favor women and children, but many of the men who survived the disaster escaped in these boats, particularly the collapsibles. Men were still trying to untether the last two collapsibles while the ship sank beneath their feet.

The *Titanic*'s hull, under great stress, began to crack. Then the entire ship broke in two. Terrified passengers fastened their life jackets and leapt into the water. The *Titanic*'s flooded bow section sank quickly. After a harrowing wait, the ship's stern began to tilt and take on water.

Rowing away from the *Titanic*, lifeboat passengers could see the ship's hundreds of electric lights suddenly blink out. A moment later they heard a noise "like an immense heap of gravel being tipped from a height" as the ship's stern reared up and everything inside—furniture, fittings, machinery—crashed out of place.[6] The ship went down, plunging into the dark ocean.

Why Did the Titanic Break in Half?

As the *Titanic* sank, its hull tore into two pieces. The bow of the ship had been flooding for nearly three hours when it was pulled underwater, causing the ship to tilt. The ship's stern, rising out of the water, was extremely heavy and not built to withstand this type of pressure. The bow forced the stern upward while gravity pulled the stern downward. Finally, the ship split in two at a natural weak point between the third and fourth funnels. The steel plates that made up the hull tore apart, allowing the ship's stern to settle back onto its keel. The bow of the ship sank while water began to flood into the open end of the stern. Within a few minutes, the stern was sinking as well, tilted nearly perpendicular to the surface of the ocean. It sank vertically, with the ship's propellers high in the air.

Desperate passengers clambered up the deck and clung onto the railings. Then, they stepped out into the ocean.

In the silence that followed, a moan rose over the water, a collective cry for help from hundreds of people freezing to death. "They told me the people in the water were singing, but I knew they were screaming," remembered Violet Mellinger, who was 13 years old at the time of the disaster.[7]

 # The  World.

Weather Forecast: UNSETTLED. "Circulation Books Open to All." "Circulation Books Open to All." Weather Forecast: UNSETTLED.

VOL. LII. NO. 18,501. ★ Copyright, 1912, by The Press Publishing Co. (The New York World). NEW YORK, TUESDAY, APRIL 16, 1912. •• PRICE | ONE CENT in Greater New York and Jersey City. / TWO CENTS outside of Greater New York, Jersey City and on trains.

GREAT TITANIC SINKS; MORE THAN 1.500 LOST; 866 WOMEN AND CHILDREN KNOWN TO BE SAVED; SCORES OF NOTABLES NOT ACCOUNTED FOR

THE LOST LINER, HER POSITION AND THAT OF OTHER SHIPS WHEN SHE HIT ICEBERG

The TITANIC
LENGTH—882 FT.
BEAM—92 FT.
DEPTH—94 FT.
DISPLACEMENT 45,000 TONS
VALUE (ESTIMATED) $10,000,000

WHITE LINES ON SIDE OF STEAMSHIP INDICATE LOCATION of BULKHEADS...

(1) "VIRGINIAN" 170 MILES from SCENE of the COLLISION, STEAMS to her AID and IS the FIRST VESSEL to REACH SPOT.
(2) "CARPATHIA" (3) BALTIC (4) "OLYMPIC" (5) "PARISIAN" and (6) "CALIFORNIA" ALL PUT on FULL STEAM to REACH STRICKEN BOAT
(7) "CARPATHIA" TAKES PASSENGERS from LIFE BOATS and PUTS BACK for NEW YORK.

600 MILES

Where TITANIC STRUCK ICEBERG 10.25 P.M. SUNDAY LONG. 50°14' WEST LAT. 41-46 NORTH

White Star Official Admits the Greatest Disaster in Marine History — J. J. Astor Rumored Lost, but Bride Saved — Text of Olympic's Fateful Message—Partial List Is Received.

HOPE THAT MANY WILL BE FOUND ON WRECKAGE.

Virginian and Parisian Reach Scene Too Late— They Are Joined by Other Steamers, Which Find Only Debris—Capt. Smith Believed to Have Gone Down with Ship—The Saved Suffer Severely from Exposure, After Floating in the Lifeboats for Eight Hours.

More than fifteen hundred souls, men, women and children, were lost, it is feared, in the wreck of the White Star liner Titanic, latest and greatest ship of the seas, which collided with an iceberg at 10.25 P. M. Sunday night and sank off the Banks of Newfoundland at 2.20 A. M. yesterday, less than four hours after she had struck.

Capt. Haddock of the Olympic sent this despatch by wireless to the White Star line last evening:

"Carpathia reached Titanic position at daybreak. Found boats and wreckage only. Titanic sank about 2.20 A. M., in 41.46 North, 50.14 West. All her boats accounted for, containing about 675 souls saved, crew and passengers included. Nearly all saved women and children. Leyland liner Californian remained and searching exact position of disaster. LOSS LIKELY TOTAL 1,800 SOULS.

The exact text of this despatch was closely guarded until after midnight by Vice-President Franklin of the White Star line, who received it at 7 o'clock. It gave the first definite news of the sinking of the Titanic and of the great loss of life.

But it is believed that the words "loss likely total 1,800 souls" is an error due to the ignorance of Capt. Haddock and the rescued passengers of the total number of persons aboard.

There were, according to the ship's manifest, 325 first cabin, 285 second cabin, and 710 steerage, a total of 1,320 passengers, and a crew of 860. This would make 2,180 persons aboard and some late comers not on the passenger lists are believed to have brought the total up to 2,200. Deducting 675 from this, the lost would only number 1,505, which Mr. Franklin believes to be correct.

A wireless despatch from the Olympic was picked up by a Boston operator late last night, in which it was stated that the Carpathia was on her way to New York with 866 passengers rescued from the Titanic. The rescued, the despatch read, were mostly women and children, and the despatch concluded:

"Grave fears are felt for the safety of the balance of the passengers and crew."

The disparity between this number of rescued, 866, and the 675 mentioned in Capt. Haddock's despatch to the White Star line was explained on the theory that the Carpathia might have picked up some more passengers in lifeboats after the Olympic had sent her first message to the White Star line. Nothing to confirm this, however, was obtainable.

TO THE RESCUE

Alone on the North Atlantic Ocean, many of the survivors of the *Titanic* were in shock. Within three hours, their entire lives had changed forever. Few of them even knew whether help was on the way.

In the Lifeboats

All of the *Titanic*'s 20 lifeboats had been launched, though the last two collapsibles were washed off the ship as it sank and served more as rafts than boats. Most of the lifeboats were rowed swiftly away from the sinking ship, as the crew feared the small boats would be sucked underwater if they remained nearby. By the time the *Titanic* disappeared underwater, its lifeboats were scattered across a wide area.

How Did the Titanic Victims Die?

Contrary to a common assumption, the majority of the passengers and crew who died in the shipwreck did not drown. In fact, most of them wore life jackets that kept them afloat. Hypothermia was their cause of death. On the night of the collision, the ocean water temperature was below freezing, and the feeling of hitting it was described as being stabbed by a thousand knives. In such cold water, the human body begins to shut down nonessential functions. Within 15 minutes of being in the water, the victims would have lost consciousness. After 45 minutes in the water, most of the victims would have frozen to death. Others who jumped from the ship may have broken their necks on impact or suffered heart attacks from the shock of the cold water.

The darkness of the night made it difficult to navigate once the *Titanic*'s lights were gone. While some of the lifeboats were close enough that people in the water could see and swim toward them, most were not. On the distant lifeboats, arguments broke out about whether or not it was safe to return and search for survivors in the water. Many crew members and passengers feared that if they rowed back, their boats would be swarmed by panicked swimmers and overturned. Ultimately, only two lifeboats tried to pick up people out of the water. Several other boats rowed through the ice field, searching and calling out, unsure how far they were from the wreck site.

In command of lifeboat 14, Fifth Officer Harold Lowe managed to locate several other boats and moor them all together with rope. Distributing his passengers into the other boats, he and his crew returned to the wreck site to search for survivors. By this time, an hour after the *Titanic* had sunk, they found few people left alive. They pulled four men from the water, one of whom died in the lifeboat. There was little the survivors could do but wait and hope that another ship had heard the *Titanic*'s distress calls.

The Missed Call

Just ten miles (16 km) away across the ice field, to the north of the lifeboats, the cargo ship *Californian* lay at anchor. Encountering scattered icebergs the previous evening, the captain had ordered an emergency stop and then anchored for the night rather than risk navigating in the dark. The Marconi wireless operator on board sent an ice warning to ships within range but operators on the *Titanic* were too busy with passenger messages to receive it. The *Californian*'s wireless operator went to bed shortly before the *Titanic*'s collision occurred.

Later that night, the officers on duty noticed rockets in the sky to the south of their ship. Unsure whether these were distress signals, the second officer woke the captain to report the incident. The captain, believing the *Titanic* had received his warning and steered clear of the ice field, decided it was too risky to investigate the area before dawn. He assumed the mystery ship sending the signals simply needed repairs and could be assisted in the morning. This was a tragic missed connection. Whether the *Californian* could have saved the *Titanic* is speculation,

A Distress Signal or Just a Rocket?

During the investigations into the wreck, both British and American officials strongly condemned the *Californian* for not responding to the *Titanic*'s distress signal. The officials assumed that the rockets fired into the sky by officers on the *Titanic* were easily identifiable as a distress signal, which may not have been the case. According to the system used at the time, a distress signal was defined strictly by the interval at which rockets were fired. Unless a ship's rockets were set off at an even pace of one per minute, they would not be considered a signal of distress. The *Titanic* fired at least eight rockets over the course of an hour, but whether they were set off at the correct interval remains unclear.[1]

however, since there were many factors that contributed to the misunderstanding.

Full Steam Ahead

Fifty-eight miles (93 km) to the east, the *Carpathia* was already on its way toward the *Titanic*. The ship had been traveling from New York on a journey to the Mediterranean when the wireless operator picked up the *Titanic*'s distress calls. Turning the ship from its route, Captain Arthur Rostron prepared the *Carpathia* to rescue the survivors, unsure how many there would be. As the ship steamed at top speed toward the last known position of the ocean liner, Rostron ordered lights to be posted at the gangways, rope ladders and slings to be lowered into the lifeboats, and blankets and hot coffee to be put on deck.

An hour and a half after the *Titanic* sank, the *Carpathia* approached its position. The night was still dark, but dawn was visible on the horizon. Somewhere ahead, Rostron could see a green light flare from time to time. He ordered rockets fired to communicate that help was near and doubled the lookouts to watch for icebergs. Following the green light, the ship slowed only once lifeboat 2 had come into view. From the lifeboat far below, Fourth Officer Boxhall called for the captain of the *Carpathia* to take them on board.

As dawn broke, the survivors could finally see the large ice field and the other lifeboats straggled across the water. Some of the boats had drifted several miles away, while others huddled together. Far away on lifeboat six, Quartermaster Robert Hichens, who was at the *Titanic*'s wheel during the collision, refused to row toward the *Carpathia*. He had been in a terrible temper all night and was convinced the ship would not rescue them. Angered by Hichens's pessimism, first-class passenger Margaret Brown overruled him, organizing several women and men to take control of the oars. Over the next several hours, other distant lifeboats also crept

Rescue Timeline

⚓ 12:25 a.m.—The *Carpathia* receives a distress call from the *Titanic*.

⚓ 2:10 a.m.—The *Carpathia* receives its last message from the *Titanic*.

⚓ 2:20 a.m.—The *Titanic* sinks.

⚓ 4:10 a.m.—The *Carpathia* reaches the last position of the *Titanic*.

⚓ 8:30 a.m.—The *Carpathia* rescues the last lifeboat passengers.

⚓ 8:50 a.m.—The *Carpathia* leaves the *Titanic* wreck site.

closer to the *Carpathia* and waited their turn to be saved. As the sun rose, the survivors of the *Titanic* slowly climbed or were lifted on board the *Carpathia*.

On the Carpathia

As the dazed survivors boarded the *Carpathia*, they were met with offers of blankets, food, and hot drinks. Three doctors treated the injured while several *Carpathia* passengers volunteered their cabins for women who had lost their husbands. Supervising the scene, Captain Rostron noticed how quiet and exhausted the survivors were. He later recollected, "The rescued came solemnly, dumbly, out of a shivering shadow."[2]

By 8:30 a.m., after four hours of work, the last survivors were brought on board the *Carpathia*. Women who had clung to the ship's railings scanning each new lifeboat for their husbands had to accept that the men were not coming. A funeral service was held and then, five hours after the rescue ship had arrived, the *Carpathia* slowly steamed away from the site of the *Titanic*'s grave.

Bruce Ismay, who had climbed aboard one of the *Titanic*'s last lifeboats, was resting in the *Carpathia*'s doctor's cabin. He seemed to be in a state of severe shock, though the doctor had given him a dose of opium to calm his nerves—a common sedative at the time. Rostron visited him to determine a plan for the survivors, and together they decided the safest course was to return to New York, where the *Titanic*'s passengers had expected to dock.

On deck, many survivors continued to search for their family and friends, while others settled down to sleep on the floors of the dining room and lounge. In the Marconi room, the wireless operator worked all day and all night transmitting messages. On the empty ocean, the *Carpathia* turned and sailed toward New York.

⚓ *Crowds waited in New York City for* Titanic *survivors to arrive.*

Chapter 10

LEGACY OF THE SHIPWRECK

On the evening of April 18, the New York docks were crowded with thousands of onlookers as the *Carpathia* steamed slowly into port. The sky was dark, and it was raining, but camera flashbulbs popped and flared as the ocean liner drew nearer. Police officers held back the tense family members and excited reporters until the passengers could disembark. For the survivors of the *Titanic* disaster, their lives in the spotlight were just beginning.

In the Media

Days earlier on the morning of April 15, when the first news of the shipwreck began to trickle into New York, few people knew what to believe. Conflicting reports came in over the wireless from different ships, and even the vice president of the White Star Line could not receive a definite answer about the state of the *Titanic*. Newspapers, however, needed to publish, and each of them picked a story to sell, with most headlines remaining hopeful.

One story that took hold was that the *Titanic* had been damaged in the collision and was being towed to Halifax, Canada, by the *Virginian*. The White Star Line believed the story that first day, even chartering a train to transport passengers from Halifax to New York, until employees finally received a message from the captain of the *Olympic* confirming that the *Titanic* had sunk. It was a shocking conclusion to a day of anxious uncertainty.

In the days that followed, media in New York, London, and Paris exploded with bizarre stories that had no basis in reality. Headlines claimed the *Titanic*'s survivors were all in comas or had gone insane, that Italians on board had been shot, and that one passenger's pet pig had been rescued. By the time the *Carpathia* docked in New York, reporters were ravenous for new stories, some of them hounding survivors as they searched for their families in the crowd.

NOTHING ON EARTH
COULD COME BETWEEN THEM.

LEONARDO DiCaprio KATE WINSLET

TITANIC

Titanic in ⚓
Pop Culture⚓

In large part, the *Titanic* is still remembered due to the many books and movies about the disaster. In 1955, the book *A Night to Remember* by Walter Lord was released. It was the story of the shipwreck drawn from interviews with survivors and testimony from the investigation hearings. The book drove a new generation of interest in the *Titanic* and was adapted into a popular movie. In 1960, the musical *The Unsinkable Molly Brown*, a fictionalized account of the life of Margaret Brown, opened on Broadway, where it ran for two years. It was adapted into a 1964 movie starring actress Debbie Reynolds. In 1985, the *Titanic* story again caught the public's imagination after the discovery of the ship's wreckage. A string of documentaries and books produced throughout the 1980s and 1990s created a small industry of *Titanic* media. In 1997, the fictional movie *Titanic* was released and became wildly popular, earning more than $1 billion worldwide and collecting many awards.[1]

⚓ *Kate Winslet and Leonardo DiCaprio starred in the 1997 movie* Titanic.

Many survivors sold their accounts of the shipwreck to newspapers and magazines for hundreds of dollars.

Tales both true and false of the *Titanic*'s heroes filled the press for days. But as the public began to look for someone to blame for this unimaginable disaster, the media offered villains. Although Bruce Ismay, the highest-ranking White Star Line official to survive, helped evacuate passengers, he was publicly shamed for taking a spot in one of the last lifeboats. Before the *Titanic* set sail, he had boasted about the ship in a way that now appeared arrogant and dangerous. One newspaper called him "Brute" Ismay and blamed him for the collision.[2] The media frenzy surrounding the *Titanic* disaster was unlike anything the world had seen before.

The Investigations

Within days of the *Titanic* disaster, both British and American investigations into the cause of the collision were planned. Senator William Alden Smith of Michigan, in charge of the American hearings, was determined to discover whether the White Star Line had sacrificed the safety of the ship. His questions to witnesses often focused on who was to blame for the wreck. Lord Mersey, head of the British investigation, was interested in safety as well, but he avoided accusations. His questions were meant to reveal the facts of the collision while allowing the British Board of Trade to remain above criticism.

In the American investigation, as in its media, Bruce Ismay was targeted as the source of the *Titanic* disaster. In addition to his responsibility as chairman of the White Star Line, several witnesses testified that they had heard him talk about his pride in the speed the *Titanic* was achieving. The ship's speed was a significant factor in the collision. Ocean liners slowed down only when they spotted ice, and there is little evidence that Ismay influenced Captain Smith's orders.

The British investigation was, by contrast, uninterested in blaming White Star Line officials. In fact, many people believed that the hearings whitewashed the shipwreck, allowing the company and the Board of Trade to avoid responsibility for safety problems. Whether or not this is true, both investigations produced similar recommendations for new ship safety laws based on the testimonies given and evidence gathered.

Third Sister Ship

The White Star Line's third sister ship to the *Olympic* and the *Titanic* was already under construction in Belfast when the American investigation into the *Titanic*'s sinking began. In response to the investigation's final report, the *Britannic* was reinforced with a double bottom and sides as well as taller watertight bulkheads. Space was added to launch six lifeboats at a time. The ship was launched in 1914, but before its maiden voyage could take place, it was requisitioned for service as a hospital ship in World War I. While sailing in the Aegean Sea in 1916, the *Britannic* reportedly struck a mine and sank. Most of the passengers were saved.

⚓ *US Senate investigations into the sinking of the* Titanic *began at the Waldorf-Astoria Hotel in New York City on April 19, 1912.*

Technology and Safety Advances

The most significant findings of the *Titanic* investigations led to the creation of new safety and technology regulations. Shipping lanes—the highways of the Atlantic Ocean—were adjusted farther south of areas known to contain icebergs. Electric searchlights mounted on ships' bows were recommended to raise visibility at night. Laws regarding iceberg reports, distress signal rockets, and watertight bulkheads were all updated.

In perhaps the single most important update, ships were required to carry enough lifeboats to accommodate all people on board. Crew members were required to be trained in how to load and launch the boats. Each boat was assigned its own crew, and emergency drills were conducted on a regular schedule. It was also recommended that passengers be assigned to the boats nearest their cabins.

Regulations were established for the use of Marconi wireless on ships, which had previously been treated as a profit-making business. Now, ships were required to have a wireless operator on duty 24 hours a day in order to communicate all messages received, with priority for navigation. Updated long-range wireless sets were installed in new ships, as well as telephones so that wireless operators could speak to officers on the ship's bridge without leaving their stations. International standards for wireless communication were implemented as the technology's vital role in a disaster situation was finally understood.

The Survivors

Out of some 2,200 passengers and crew, approximately 710 survived.[3] Conflicting passenger lists make exact numbers impossible to know. Of the almost 900 crew members, only just over 200 survived.[4] For the *Titanic*'s survivors, investigations and regulations could not change what they had experienced. Whether Captain Smith, Bruce Ismay, First Officer Murdoch, or anyone

Will the Titanic *Ever* Be Raised?

Although the wreck of the *Titanic* has been explored, it's unlikely it will ever be raised. For more than 100 years, the ship has lain in total darkness deep on the ocean floor, broken into two huge pieces. In that time, it has deteriorated. At the shipwreck's depth of more than 12,000 feet (3,700 m), water pressure is extremely strong, making movement difficult and dangerous.[6] Attempting to raise the ship could damage it further. However, explorers using submersibles have salvaged many artifacts from the wreckage, as well as one piece of the ship's hull. It's possible that other pieces could be raised in the future as better underwater excavation technology is developed.

at all was to blame, large parts of people's lives were buried at the bottom of the ocean. Many of them never fully recovered from the loss. Others had trouble finding words to speak about what they experienced as the ship sank. Violet Mellinger, 13 years old at the time, later tried to describe how it happened. "It just went down," she explained without embellishment. "It was gone."[5]

The bareness of this testimony reveals the struggle many survivors had in accepting the tragedy. The *Titanic* had been unsinkable—and then it sank. The legacy of the shipwreck remains bound up in ideas of punishment for arrogance and pride, but the ship was never doomed. Ultimately, the *Titanic* was a ship like any other, and people made mistakes that led to a disaster. After it sank, many survivors carried that difficult knowledge with them for the rest of their lives.

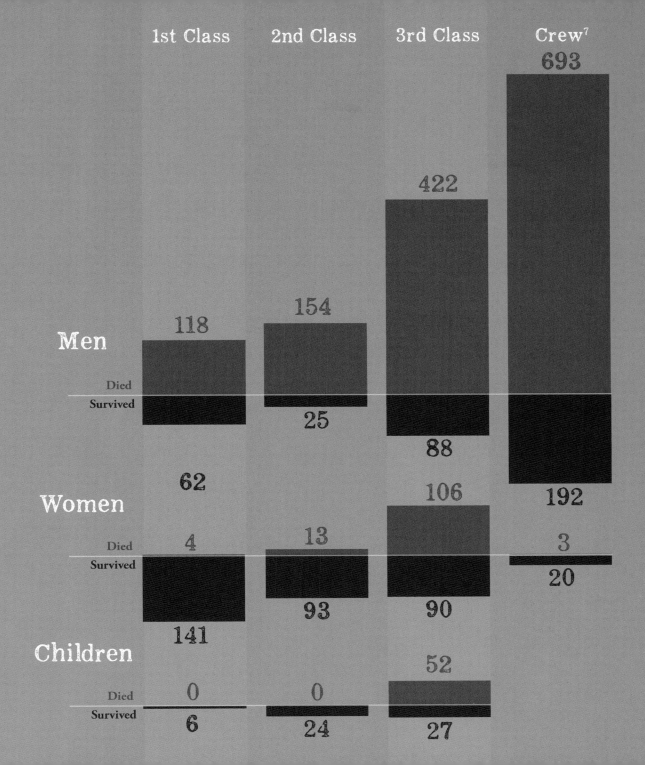

Timeline

1837

- ⚓ The first steamship built for service on the North Atlantic Ocean launches.

1840

- ⚓ The Cunard Line, founded by Samuel Cunard, launches its first ships.

1868

- ⚓ Thomas Ismay takes ownership of the White Star Line.

1884

- ⚓ Charles Parsons invents the steam turbine.

1889

- ⚓ The White Star Line launches the world's first modern ocean liners.

1899

- ⚓ Bruce Ismay becomes chairman of the White Star Line.

1902

- ⚓ J. P. Morgan adds the White Star Line to his shipping conglomerate.

1907

- ⚓ The Cunard Line launches the *Lusitania* and the *Mauretania*, the largest ships in the world.
- ⚓ The White Star Line begins plans for the *Olympic*, the *Titanic*, and a third unnamed ship.

1908

- ⚓ The White Star Line begins construction of the *Olympic*.

1909

‡ The White Star Line begins construction of the *Titanic*.

1911

‡ The *Olympic* completes its maiden voyage; the White Star Line launches the *Titanic*.

1912

‡ On April 10, the *Titanic* begins its maiden voyage from Southampton, England.

‡ On April 14, the *Titanic* strikes an iceberg.

‡ On April 15, the *Titanic* sinks, and its survivors are rescued by the *Carpathia*.

‡ On April 18, the *Carpathia* arrives in New York.

1914

‡ The White Star Line launches the *Britannic*.

1934

‡ The Cunard Line buys the White Star Line.

1985

‡ Dr. Robert Ballard discovers the site of the *Titanic*'s wreckage.

Essential Facts

What Happened

The ocean liner *Titanic*, reputed to be unsinkable, sank after striking an iceberg that damaged its hull. Several of the wealthiest people in the world traveled on the *Titanic*, including J. J. Astor, who died in the shipwreck. The ship carried enough life jackets for everyone on board but only enough lifeboats for one-half of the passengers.

When It Happened

The *Titanic* sank on the early morning of April 15, 1912.

Where It Happened

The *Titanic* sank in the North Atlantic Ocean.

Key Players

- Bruce Ismay was the chairman of the White Star Line, the company that owned the *Titanic*.
- Lord William Pirrie was the chairman of Harland and Wolff, the company that built the *Titanic*.
- Thomas Andrews was Harland and Wolff's chief architect, and he designed the *Titanic*.
- Edward Smith was the captain of the *Titanic*.
- William Murdoch was the *Titanic*'s first officer, who was in command at the time of the collision.
- Fred Fleet was the *Titanic*'s lookout at the time of the collision.

Legacy

The investigation of the shipwreck led to the strengthening of ship safety regulations and the improvement of wireless communication technology. The sinking of the *Titanic* has captivated the collective imagination for more than a century. The event continues to loom large in popular culture through documentaries and movies.

Quote

"I cannot conceive of any vital disaster happening to this vessel. Modern shipbuilding has gone beyond that."

—Edward Smith, captain of the Titanic

Glossary

bow

The forward part of a ship; the point that is most forward when the ship is under way.

bulkhead

Any of the partition walls used for subdividing the interior of a ship into compartments. The main partition walls also serve to strengthen the ship's structure and protect against water passing from one compartment to another.

financier

A specialist in finance and especially in the financing of businesses.

gangway

Place of entrance to or exit from a ship.

gantry

An elevated crane structure with hoisting gear designed to travel along rails on the ground level.

hull

The frame or body of a ship, excluding masts, sails, and rigging.

Industrial Revolution

The rapid development of industry that occurred in Britain in the late 1700s and 1800s and migrated to the United States, brought about by the introduction of machinery.

keel

A center line running along the bottom of a ship for strength, often referred to as the backbone.

maiden voyage

The first trip a ship makes after it has been launched and passed its sea trials.

piston

A part of an engine that moves up and down inside a tube, causing other parts of the engine to move.

port

A harbor town or city where ships may take on or discharge cargo or passengers; the left side of a ship when looking forward.

quartermaster

An officer on a ship who steers the wheel and has charge of the navigating instruments.

requisition

Demand for use by military authorities for supplies or other needs.

rivet

Pin used for connecting two or more pieces of material by passing it through a drilled or punched hole and hammering down one or both ends.

slipway

A space in a shipyard where there is a foundation for launching and that is occupied by a ship while under construction.

starboard

The right side of a ship when looking forward.

steerage

The least desirable accommodations for passengers, which are occupied by people paying the lowest fares.

stern

The rear part of a ship; the farthest part from the bow.

submersible

A small vehicle that can operate underwater, used especially for research.

turbine

An engine with a central driving shaft that is fitted with a series of winglike parts that are spun by the pressure of water, steam, or gas.

victual

Supply or provision of food, often for traveling.

Additional Resources

Selected Bibliography

Barratt, Nick. *Lost Voices from the* Titanic*: The Definitive Oral History*. New York: Palgrave Macmillan, 2010. Print.

Davenport-Hines, Richard. *Voyagers of the* Titanic*: Passengers, Sailors, Shipbuilders, Aristocrats, and the Worlds They Came From*. New York: HarperCollins, 2012. Print.

Lynch, Donald, and Ken Marschall. Titanic*: An Illustrated History*. Toronto, ON: Madison, 1995. Print.

Further Readings

Hancock, Claire. *The* Titanic *Notebook: The Story of the World's Most Famous Ship*. San Rafael, CA: Insight, 2012. Print.

Hopkinson, Deborah. Titanic*: Voices from the Disaster*. New York: Scholastic, 2014. Print.

Wolf, Allan. *The Watch That Ends the Night: Voices from the* Titanic. Somerville, MA: Candlewick, 2013. Print.

Online Resources

Booklinks
NONFICTION NETWORK
FREE! ONLINE NONFICTION RESOURCES

To learn more about the *Titanic*, visit **abdobooklinks.com**. These links are routinely monitored and updated to provide the most current information available.

More Information

For more information on this subject, contact or visit the following organizations:

Maritime Museum of the Atlantic

1675 Lower Water Street
Halifax, Nova Scotia, Canada
B3J 1S3
902-424-7490
maritimemuseum.novascotia.ca

The Maritime Museum of the Atlantic's *Titanic* exhibit includes artifacts, reproductions of the *Titanic*'s furniture, and a model of one of the lifeboats.

Titanic Historical Society & Museum

208 Main Street
Indian Orchard, MA 01151
413-543-4770
titanichistoricalsociety.org

The *Titanic* Historical Society & Museum features artifacts from the *Titanic* and items from survivors.

Source Notes

Chapter 1. Abandon Ship!

1. Donald Lynch and Ken Marschall. Titanic: *An Illustrated History*. Toronto: Madison Books, 1995. Print. 93.

2. Charlotte Collyer. "How I Was Saved from the *Titanic*." *San Francisco Call* 2 June 1912. *Click Americana*. Web. 14 May 2017.

3. Ibid.

4. Ibid.

5. Ibid.

6. Ibid.

7. *Encyclopedia Titanica*. Encyclopedia Titanica, 1 Sept. 1996. Web. 28 Apr. 2017.

Chapter 2. The Growth of the Ocean Liner

1. Michael Davie. Titanic: *The Death and Life of a Legend*. New York: Knopf, 1987. Print. 6.

2. Ibid. 9.

3. Michael Davie. Titanic: *The Death and Life of a Legend*. New York: Knopf, 1987. Print. 11.

4. "Cunard Line Archives." *National Archives*. National Archives, n.d. Web. 11 May 2017.

5. Ibid. 13.

Chapter 3. Building the *Titanic*

1. *"Mr. Thomas Andrews Jr." Encyclopedia Titanica*. Encyclopedia Titanica, 25 Aug. 2017. Web. 11 May 2017.

2. Donald Lynch and Ken Marschall. Titanic: *An Illustrated History*. Toronto: Madison Books, 1995. Print. 19.

3. "Deaths of Shipyard Workers." *Encyclopedia Titanica*. Encyclopedia Titanica, 2017. Web. 11 May 2017.

4. "*Titanic*: Building the Largest Moving Object in History." *Ultimate Titanic*. Ultimate Titanic, 2012. Web. 28 Apr. 2017.

5. Ibid.

6. "*Titanic*'s "Brittle" Steel?" *Titanic Historical Society*. Titanic Historical Society, 2014. Web. 28 Apr. 2017.

7. Tim Maltin. *101 Things You Thought You Knew about the Titanic . . . but Didn't!* New York: Penguin, 2011. Print. 9.

8. Ibid. 11.

9. "*Titanic*'s "Brittle" Steel?" *Titanic Historical Society*. Titanic Historical Society, 2014. Web. 28 Apr. 2017.

10. Michael Davie. Titanic: *The Death and Life of a Legend*. New York: Knopf, 1987. Print. 17.

11. "*Titanic*: Building the Largest Moving Object in History." *Ultimate Titanic*. Ultimate Titanic, 2012. Web. 28 Apr. 2017.

Chapter 4. Inside the *Titanic*

1. Donald Lynch and Ken Marschall. Titanic: *An Illustrated History*. Toronto: Madison Books, 1995. Print. 23.

2. "Machinery." Titanic *Research & Modeling Association*. *Titanic* Research & Modeling Association, *1999*. Web. 28 Apr. 2017.

3. "*Titanic*: By the Numbers." *Ultimate Titanic*. Ultimate Titanic, 2012. Web. 28 Apr. 2017.

4. Ibid.

5. Michael Davie. Titanic: *The Death and Life of a Legend*. New York: Knopf, 1987. Print. 15.

6. "*Titanic*: Launch and Sea Trials." *Ultimate Titanic*. Ultimate Titanic, 2012. Web. 28 Apr. 2017.

7. "Map of the *Titanic*'s Maiden and Final Voyage." *Denver Post*. Denver Post, 2 May 2016. Web. 16 May 2017.

8. Dave Fowler. "*Titanic* Crew." *Titanic Facts*. History in Numbers, 2011. Web. 16 May 2017.

Chapter 5. Bon Voyage

1. Dave Fowler. "*Titanic* Passengers." *Titanic Facts*. History in Numbers, 2011. Web. 16 May 2017.

2. "*Titanic*: By the Numbers." *Ultimate Titanic*. Ultimate Titanic, 2012. Web. 28 Apr. 2017.

3. "Cargo Manifest." *Encyclopedia Titanica*. Encyclopedia Titanica, 2017. Web. 11 May 2017.

4. Ibid.

5. Donald Lynch and Ken Marschall. Titanic: *An Illustrated History*. Toronto: Madison Books, 1995. Print. 33–35.

6. Ibid.

Source Notes Continued

Chapter 6. On the Open Ocean

1. "*Titanic*: By the Numbers." *Ultimate Titanic*. Ultimate Titanic, 2012. Web. 28 Apr. 2017.

2. Ibid.

3. Megan Garber. "The Technology That Allowed the *Titanic* Survivors to Survive." *Atlantic*. Atlantic Media Company, 13 Apr. 2012. Web. 2 May 2017.

4. Hugh Brewster. *Gilded Lives, Fatal Voyage: The* Titanic's *First-Class Passengers and Their World*. New York: Crown, 2012. Print. 107–108.

5. Tim Maltin. *101 Things You Thought You Knew about the* Titanic . . . *but Didn't!* New York: Penguin, 2011. Print. 65–66.

6. Richard Davenport-Hines. *Voyagers of the* Titanic: *Passengers, Sailors, Shipbuilders, Aristocrats, and the Worlds They Came From*. New York: HarperCollins, 2012. Print. 132.

7. Hugh Brewster. *Gilded Lives, Fatal Voyage: The* Titanic's *First-Class Passengers and Their World*. New York: Crown, 2012. Print. 107–108.

8. Ibid. 150.

Chapter 7. Iceberg Ahead

1. "Defending Fleet and Lee." *Encyclopedia Titanica*. Encyclopedia Titanica, 2017. Web. 11 May 2017.

2. Richard Davenport-Hines. *Voyagers of the* Titanic: *Passengers, Sailors, Shipbuilders, Aristocrats, and the Worlds They Came From*. New York: HarperCollins, 2012. Print. 209.

3. Ibid.

4. Donald Lynch and Ken Marschall. Titanic: *An Illustrated History*. Toronto: Madison Books, 1995. Print. 89.

5. "I Survived the Sinking of the *Titanic*." *Encyclopedia Titanica*. Encyclopedia Titanica, 2017. Web. 11 May 2017.

6. Tom Kuntz, ed. *The* Titanic *Disaster Hearings*. New York: Simon and Schuster, 1998. 423. *Google Book Search*. Web. 2 Oct. 2017.

7. Andrew Wilson. *Shadow of the* Titanic: *The Extraordinary Stories of Those Who Survived*. New York: Simon and Schuster, 2012. 227. *Google Book Search*. Web. 2 Oct. 2017.

8. John Protasio. "A Titanic Centennial." *US Naval Institute*. US Naval Institute, April 2012. Web. 2 Oct. 2017.

9. Tom Kuntz, ed. *The* Titanic *Disaster Hearings*. New York: Simon and Schuster, 1998. 369. *Google Book Search*. Web. 2 Oct. 2017.

10. Ibid. 438.

Chapter 8. Disaster

1. Donald Lynch and Ken Marschall. Titanic: *An Illustrated History*. Toronto: Madison Books, 1995. Print. 91.

2. Richard Davenport-Hines. *Voyagers of the* Titanic: *Passengers, Sailors, Shipbuilders, Aristocrats, and the Worlds They Came From*. New York: HarperCollins, 2012. Print. 213.

3. Ibid. 223–233.

4. Mikael Elinder and Oscar Erixson. "Gender, Norms and Survival in Maritime Disasters." *Proceedings of the National Academy of Sciences of the USA* 109.33 (2012): 13220–13224. *PNAS*. Web. 12 Sept. 2017.

5. "Mr. Charles Herbert Lightoller." *Encyclopedia Titanica*. Encyclopedia Titanica, 2017. Web. 12 Sept. 2017.

6. Richard Davenport-Hines. *Voyagers of the* Titanic: *Passengers, Sailors, Shipbuilders, Aristocrats, and the Worlds They Came From*. New York: HarperCollins, 2012. Print. 246–252.

7. "Miss Violet Madeline Mellinger." *Encyclopedia Titanica*. Encyclopedia Titanica, 2017. Web. 11 May 2017.

Chapter 9. To the Rescue

1. John G. Gillespie. "When Is a Rocket Called a Distress Signal or Just a Flash in the Sky?" *Titanic Historical Society*. Titanic Historical Society, 2001. Web. 28 Apr. 2017.

2. Richard Davenport-Hines. *Voyagers of the* Titanic: *Passengers, Sailors, Shipbuilders, Aristocrats, and the Worlds They Came From*. New York: HarperCollins, 2012. Print. 257.

Chapter 10. Legacy of the Shipwreck

1. "Titanic (1997)." *IMDB*. Internet Movie Database, n.d. Web. 31 May 2017.

2. Richard Davenport-Hines. *Voyagers of the* Titanic: *Passengers, Sailors, Shipbuilders, Aristocrats, and the Worlds They Came From*. New York: HarperCollins, 2012. Print. 261–291.

3. *Encyclopedia Titanica*. Encyclopedia Titanica, 1 Sept. 1996. Web. 28 Apr. 2017.

4. David Randall. "The Forgotten Victims: How the *Titanic* Tragedy Handed a Devastating Legacy to the People of Southampton." *Independent*. Independent, 4 Mar. 2012. Web. 12 Sept. 2017.

5. "Miss Violet Madeline Mellinger." *Encyclopedia Titanica*. Encyclopedia Titanica, 2017. Web. 11 May 2017.

6. Tim Maltin. *101 Things You Thought You Knew about the* Titanic . . . *but Didn't!* New York: Penguin, 2011. Print. 293–294.

7. Robert J. MacG. Dawson. "The 'Unusual Episode' Data Revisited." *Journal of Statistics Education* 3.3 (1995). *AMSTAT*. Web. 12 Sept. 2017.

Index

About the Author

Tristan Poehlmann is a freelance writer of educational nonfiction on history, science, and art. His most recent book is *The Stonewall Riots: The Fight for LGBT Rights*. A former museum exhibit developer, he holds a master's degree in writing for children and young adults from Vermont College of Fine Arts. He lives in the San Francisco Bay Area.

About the Content Consultant

Sheryl Rinkol has been studying the *Titanic* for more than 35 years. Inspired by her grandmother, she has expanded her *Titanic* interests, researching and traveling under four different grants. For three years, she developed and taught a *Titanic* class at Nebraska Wesleyan University, which was the first and only semester-long *Titanic* class. Overall, she has taught ten different *Titanic* courses ranging from summer enrichment programs for elementary children to weeklong classes for senior citizens. Her *Titanic* fascination has taken her around the world to *Titanic* exhibits, museums, and ports. Residing in Half Moon Bay, California, she is available for speaking engagements.